D1526222

LEADERSHIP'S ADVERSARY:
WINNING THE WAR BETWEEN
LEADERSHIP AND MANAGEMENT

LEADERSHIP'S ADVERSARY:
WINNING THE WAR BETWEEN LEADERSHIP AND MANAGEMENT

MICHAEL S. WADE

Nova Science Publishers, Inc.
New York

Senior Editors: Susan Boriotti and Donna Dennis

Coordinating Editor: Tatiana Shohov

Office Manager: Annette Hellinger

Graphics: Wanda Serrano

Book Production: Matthew Kozlowski, Jonathan Rose and Jennifer Vogt

Circulation: Raymond Davis, Cathy DeGregory and Ave Maria Gonzalez

Communications and Acquisitions: Serge P. Shohov

Library of Congress Cataloging-in-Publication Data

Wade, Michael.
    Leadership's adversary: winning the war between leadership and management /
Michael S. Wade.
      p. cm.
    Includes index.
    ISBN 1-59033-211-3.
      1. Leadership. 2. Management. I. Title.
HD57.7 .W295 2002
658.4—dc21

2002016613

Copyright © 2002 by Nova Science Publishers, Inc.
              227 Main Street, Suite 100
              Huntington, New York 11743
              Tele. 631-424-NOVA (6682)   Fax 631-425-5933
              E Mail: Novascience@earthlink.net
              www.novapublishers.com

Printed in the United States of America

CONTENTS

Chapter 1

THE LEADERSHIP - MANAGEMENT WAR

The Duke of Wellington, whose reputation as a great commander was secured with his victory over Napoleon at Waterloo, had a jarring experience in his early days as Britain's prime minister. After his first Cabinet meeting he noted, "An extraordinary affair. I gave them their orders and they wanted to stay and discuss them."[1]

Wellington's surprise is understandable. While commanding the redcoats, he had enjoyed an environment where subordinates raced - or appeared to race - like greyhounds to carry out his most modestly expressed desires. The prime ministership, however, propelled him into a puzzling new collegial world where a chief executive's clear and shouted instructions could have all the impact of a fistfight with a featherbed.

Wellington was no fool. He was a proven leader. He also possessed unquestionable skills as a manager. But in order to succeed as prime minister, he would have to readjust the relationship between his leadership and managerial responsibilities. This readjustment would not simply be necessary because of the different responsibilities of his new office. It would also be needed to win the hidden war waged within Wellington's professional soul and which even today divides the kindred spirits of all executives and managers: the war between leadership and management.

---

[1] Peter Hennessy, *Cabinet* (Oxford: Basil Blackwell, 1990), p.121.

This book is about that war and how leaders - and managers - can win it.

In order to understand the subtle tensions and outright conflicts, we first must examine the nature of the two disciplines. A classic distinction between leadership and management is that leaders do the right thing and managers do things right. Managers know how to get from Point A to Point B and leaders know whether it's worth the trip.[2]

That distinction also carries a warning. Neglect either responsibility and you can wind up doing the wrong thing right or the right thing wrong. If executives or managers focus solely on leadership, managerial problems can ambush their plans, as any executive who has hastily made personnel appointments can attest. But if all eyes are cast only to management, the resulting efficiency may simply push the organization more rapidly down the wrong road.

Unfortunately, society loves nifty stereotypes and so executives often are conveniently - and sloppily - labeled as leaders or managers. Although the term "manager" has a respectable usage, it suffers when juxtaposed against its more glamorous cousin. The perceived contrast turns an innocent term into a career-killer. When an executive or manager is dismissed as "a manager, not a leader," blood has just been shed.

That caste system is both harmful and inaccurate. Rather than making sharp distinctions or rating one over the other, it is far more helpful to think of leadership and management as responsibilities that are inherent in formal or informal positions of authority. A person possessing authority is ipso facto a leader *and* a manager. [In order to avoid confusion and awkwardness, henceforth I will use the term "executive" to describe one who holds both leadership and managerial responsibilities. People with the job titles of manager or supervisor should also be embraced by the term.] An executive may perform poorly as a leader or manager or both, but those responsibilities are held regardless of the performance. Many employers cling to the old caste-oriented rhetoric but unwittingly apply the more accurate approach through their performance appraisal

---

[2] Warren Bennis and Burt Nanus, *Leaders: The Strategies for Taking Charge* (New York: Harper & Row, 1985), p.40.

systems. As they evaluate executives on demonstrated leadership abilities, they acknowledge a range instead of a litmus test. The range recognizes that people can demonstrate degrees of leadership abilities just as they can with managerial ones.

This acceptance of a fluid range not only destroys false hierarchies, it better reflects the reality and chaos of the workplace. With rare exception, individuals in positions of authority do not constantly operate in neat little cubicles as either leaders or managers. When they are not acting exclusively as followers, people perform in dynamic combinations, one moment being more of a leader, the next more of a manager and on still another occasion becoming an inseparable blend of both roles, perhaps with a dash of raw power wielder tossed in. They are not "either-or." They are "both-and."

THE BATTLEFIELD

Although these changing roles can be confusing, their frequent shifts are not the only problem. Matters easily slip into chaos when well-meaning executives seek to achieve what appears to be a desirable goal: handling the full range of both responsibilities and doing the right things in the right way. The problem with this ambitious aim is leadership and management responsibilities are not just different, they actually conflict. On occasion, the exercise of one can prevent or hinder the effective exercise of the other. For example:

Leaders are expected to take bold action, even if it entails breaking some rules. Managers are supposed to follow procedures.
Leaders are expected to maintain a sense of mystery, an aura that is facilitated by keeping a prudent distance from their followers. Managers are supposed to be approachable and closely in touch with their associates.
Leaders are expected to foresee and handle a broad range of forces that can possibly affect the organization. Managers are supposed to stay within their specific area of responsibility and follow the guidance of top management.

Leaders are expected to be "good butchers" and sacrifice erring associates for the welfare of the organization. **Managers** are supposed to salvage problem employees and avoid legal challenges. **Leaders** are expected to "shake up" departments or divisions in order to get the job done. **Managers** are supposed to get the job done with a minimum of ill feeling and turmoil.

Leaders are expected to use a broad brush and avoid getting trapped in details. **Managers** are responsible for ensuring that the details are correct and that their employees are performing their jobs properly.

Leaders are expected to have a strong, unwavering vision. **Managers** are supposed to be flexible enough to achieve that vision. These opposites could be sorted out if leaders and managers were locked into separate job descriptions. They are not because that would be impossible. A person in an executive or managerial position may be more of a leader than a manager or vice-versa, but since all executives have leadership and managerial responsibilities they possess a constant tension that can push, pull and, if not handled well, ultimately confuse, demoralize and defeat. All too frequently, leadership's adversary is management and management's adversary is leadership.

FAILING IN ORDER TO SUCCEED

The impact of this conflict should not be underestimated. The fact that executives cannot, under all circumstances, attend to or reconcile both sets of responsibilities means they must, on occasion, sacrifice the responsibilities of one role in order to meet the demands of the other. In implementing this strategy of calculated failure, an executive may wisely choose to perform in a manner that would be regarded as ineffective, inefficient, or inept if judged by management standards because, by doing so, a leadership goal is furthered. It also means an executive may, with equal wisdom, choose to botch a leadership standard in order to attain a managerial goal.

Great executives throughout history have had to resolve the clash points within and between their leadership and managerial responsibilities. The most effective executives have willingly made sacrifices because of inner certainty about their ultimate goals and the sacrifices required to achieve those goals. This process is seldom pretty, but it can produce extraordinary results. Journalist Malcolm Muggeridge, who studied Charles De Gaulle's maneuvers as the commander of the Free French led his troubled nation throughout the Second World War, concluded De Gaulle "was like . . . one of those circus clowns who ride a bicycle clumsily into the ring, seeming always to fall off, until you realize that they are in fact consummate riders, who will always recover their balance and end up standing majestically on the saddle and saluting a wildly applauding audience."[3]

Executives who refuse to make the necessary leadership versus management sacrifices and who personally try to handle both responsibilities do not avoid problems. They are destined for difficulties. By failing to choose, they send mixed signals. These signals create confusion and may trigger a result far worse than if they had consciously decided to ignore either responsibility. In cases of absolute neglect, capable associates may cover for the executive. But when the executive who has not learned how to reconcile his or her responsibilities is sufficiently involved to cause problems, then such rescuers may be prevented from intervening. The inept executive may fend off all who seek to prevent disaster.

For some individuals, the necessity for choice can be unsettling. Executives like to win, yet the clash between leadership and management forces them to accommodate some amount of failure in order to achieve overall success. Furthermore, their organizations frequently peddle the old notion that you can do it all. In truth, you cannot. But you can consciously achieve a creative and mutually beneficial balance between leadership and management.

Using examples from history as well as executive suites in business and government, the following chapters will show how to achieve that balance. Three common types of executive styles - autocratic, collegial and formalistic - are explored and specific corrective actions are provided so danger zones can be avoided.

Before embarking on this journey, it is appropriate to remember the high price sometimes paid when talented executives struggle to

---

[3] Malcolm Muggeridge, *Chronicles of Wasted Time: Number 2, The Infernal Grove* (New York: William Morrow & Company Inc., 1974), p.212.

reconcile the irreconcilable differences between leadership and management. As we shall see, that price has sometimes been in blood as well as money and reputation. When organizations and individuals act with a wary and respectful knowledge of the differences between these key responsibilities, both leadership and management will benefit.

Chapter 2

THE AUTOCRATIC EXECUTIVE

Sixth century B.C.: In a Grecian cornfield Periander, the tyrant of the Corinth city state, asks his more experienced counterpart, Thrasybulus, the tyrant of Miletus, for a little career advice. Namely, Periander is concerned about how to maintain power, a question that lingers in the heart of all autocratic executives.

Without a word, Thrasybulus takes his cane and neatly whacks off the tops of those cornstalks protruding above the others.[4]

Thrasybulus' recommendation reveals the very nature of the autocratic style. Autocratic executives want to impose their will on others; indeed, the Greek origin of the word **autocrat** means "ruling by oneself."[5] In order for that happy state to be achieved, power must be hoarded and kept from slipping away to associates who are potential rivals, usurpers or blunderers. This is no easy task because there are numerous obstacles confronting the autocrat. Among the most formidable are:

The autocrat needs skilled associates to get the job done properly and the more skilled the associate, the more dangerous he or she may

---

[4] Will Durant, *The Life of Greece* (New York: Simon & Schuster, Inc., 1939), p.90; Maurice Latey, *Patterns of Tyranny* (New York: Atheneum, 1969), p.97; Jacques Bainville, *Dictators* (Port Washington: Kenniket Press Inc., 1967), p.24.
[5] *The American Heritage Dictionary of the English Language* (New York: 1975), p.89.

be to the autocrat's own status or longevity. One of the jarring aspects of autocratic workplaces is the extent to which autocrats sacrifice efficiency and effectiveness in the name of security. In the eyes of the autocrat, this is not a problem. They see themselves as indispensable guarantors of efficiency and effectiveness, full of good intentions and noble visions. In that fantasy world, any actions guaranteeing the survival of the autocrat are justified.

Autocrats are also notoriously guilty of presuming that their way is the only way and that subordinates must be closely monitored. Former ITT chairman Harold Geneen admitted, "Well, I'm no laissez-faire, let-me-know-how-things-are-in-six-months kind of guy. I want to know what's going on. I don't want some proud guy to get into his own Vietnam and suddenly hand me his resignation. Hell, his resignation couldn't bring back the ten million dollars he'd lose."[6] Geneen justified an aggressively autocratic style by describing a straw man alternative of managerial neglect. Trust is not an overused characteristic of autocrats nor is employee empowerment. Continuing their pattern of inefficiency, autocrats foster systems where some areas are micro-managed while others suffer from gross neglect.

The autocrat must design ways to elicit ideas from associates without compromising autocratic authority or subverting the belief that the autocrat deserves to hold significant power. If this information-gathering system is poorly constructed or is not implemented, the results can be ludicrous, disastrous or both. Benito Mussolini, the hapless Italian dictator who envisioned himself a great warlord, used to leave his generals behind while attending important military conferences for fear that their presence would imply a lack of knowledge on his part.[7] Compounding this error, he acted as his own translator during coordination meetings with Adolf Hitler; a practice which frequently resulted in Mussolini leaving the room with only a partial sense of what had been said.[8] Both of these practices - coupled with his arrogance - put him on the short road to disaster. Eventually

[6] Thomas S. Burns, *Tales of ITT: An Insider's Report* (Boston 1974), p.17.
[7] Denis Mack Smith, *Mussolini* (New York: Vintage Books, 1983), p.256.
[8] Paolo Monelli, *Mussolini: An Intimate Life* (London: Thames & Hudson, 1953), pp.183-184.

his associates saw through this scam and deposed him, but for many years they were fooled by his claims of superhuman knowledge.

The autocrat must create a system that does not facilitate the making of mistakes. This is the highest obstacle of all for - given time - the autocratic style is guaranteed to produce hubris, miscalculation and inefficiency; the midwives of disaster. Whenever the benchmark is organizational excellence - as opposed to individual achievement - autocrats soon encounter trouble because of the atmosphere they foster and the limitations created by the conflict between leadership and management. As shown in the following illustration of the Autocratic Management Cycle, the autocrat's management style - whether manifested by squelching dissent, limiting information, failing to appreciate the human element, embracing egotistical delusions or some other debilitating characteristic - damages the quality of the leadership decisions that shape the organization's goals or vision. Those flawed decisions in turn create management problems as subordinates seek to achieve the goals at the ground level. When those management problems surface, the autocrat doesn't adjust by becoming less autocratic. Quite the opposite. The autocrat becomes more autocratic, often criticizing subordinates for having a failure of will. At the end of the cycle, the autocratic management style that led to the problems is even worse but, with renewed vigor, it continues on its way. The overall impact is brutal: you can find old autocrats and you can find effective autocrats but you will be hard pressed to find any old, effective autocrats. Over time, the autocrat's greatest achievement is often the raw ability to survive in power. It certainly isn't a strengthened organization.

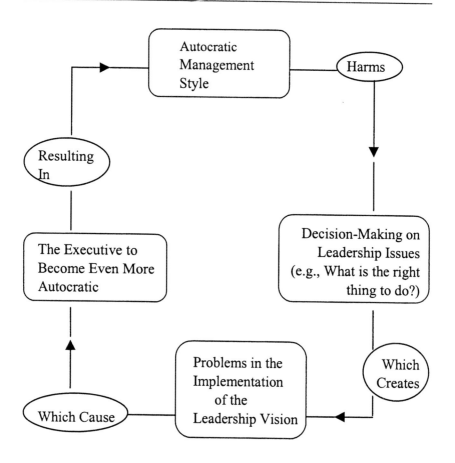

THE ARGUMENT FOR AUTOCRACY

In these days of employee empowerment and self-directed teams, autocrats are in disfavor. When times become harsh, however, their popularity surges because of the belief that undisputed leadership and strong management are needed to provide clear direction and fend off disaster. Leadership analyst Lin Bothwell equates the tendency to rely upon autocratic leadership during a crisis with an airline passenger's willingness to trust the unilateral decisions of an experienced pilot rather then the collective judgement of the manure salesmen in the back of the plane.[9]

The ancient Romans shared Bothwell's view that an autocratic approach is the best style for handling crises. In the days of their Republic, they created the position of "dictator" to deal with special dangers. Their dictators were given almost unlimited power to get the job done - with the exception of having to go to the Senate for money - but after six months their terms expired and they had to step down. As an enticement to service, dictators were immune from prosecution for actions taken while in office.[10]

Modern-day dictators, be they corporate or political, have been far less noble than the early Roman variety. Once in power, their usual concern is to consolidate or expand their regimes and few, if any, acknowledge term limits. In this chapter, we'll examine an odious autocrat, Adolf Hitler, whose extraordinary charisma created its own management problems; a very different type of autocrat, Margaret Thatcher, who operated in a noncharismatic manner within a system that was both hostile to women and designed to promote collective decision making; and finally, Winston Churchill, whose greatness as a leader was achieved because of a willingness to curb his autocratic tendencies.

A special note is appropriate before discussing Hitler. Those who are repulsed by any examination of Hitler's "management style" should recognize that studying the Nazi leader's approach permits us to examine the ethical danger signs that exist in any organization. We are accustomed to dismissing dictators and their corporate equivalents as monsters, people who would automatically repel any but the morally myopic. That comic book portrayal ignores the complexity of such individuals and the nature of their hold over others. One of Hitler's more repentant [or more manipulative] associates later observed, "One seldom recognizes the devil when he is putting his hand on your shoulder."[11] I am not of the school of thought that says

[9] Lin Bothwell, *The Art of Leadership* (New York: Prentice Hall Press,1983), pp.177-178.

[10] Will Durant, *Caesar and Christ* (New York: Simon and Schuster, 1944), pp.30-34; Bainville, pp.35-36.

[11] Albert Speer, *Inside The Third Reich* (New York: The Macmillan Company, 1970).

"The system made Hitler do it." The techniques he used, however, bolstered his ability to lead and manage in a thoroughly deceptive manner. The more we learn of such things, the better prepared we shall be to prevent them.

ADOLF HITLER CREATES FOLIE A DEUX

Adolf Hitler's rule was not based on a constitution or the authority of an office or his competence or fear; instead, its bedrock was Hitler's extraordinary charisma.

Here was a man who, despite having spent part of his adult life as a tramp on the streets of Vienna, became Chancellor of Germany at the age of forty-three. Prior to achieving the status of a world leader, he had held no executive or managerial positions other than being a corporal in the German Army and the head of the National Socialist German Workers', or Nazi, political party.

Hitler's leadership and management system revolved around the Fuhrerprinzip, or the Leader Principle, a Germanic concept of leadership in which the "Fuhrer" was believed to possess an unusual link with the persona and divinity of the people. For followers of the Fuhrerprinzip, Hitler's decisions were not subject to traditional boundaries such as logic or reason; they instead stemmed from a special sense not available to the masses or even to the Fuhrer's close associates. He could consult his advisors and study reports but, in the end, the Fuhrer would have such an extraordinary feel for the people's interests that his decisions would possess far more merit than those of an ordinary person.[12] [Those who might scoff at such simplemindedness should consider the somber attention that is commonly accorded the most banal utterances of any Fortune 500 chief executive officer.]

The Fuhrerprinzip was not some handy lore dusted off and promoted by Hitler to expand his own power, although he was not above such opportunism. It perfectly matched his natural inclinations

[12] Adolf Hitler, *Mein Kampf* (New York: Reynol & Hitchcock, 1940), p.117.

toward leadership and management. During the Second World War, American Intelligence produced a chillingly accurate description of Hitler's intuitive style:

> "[Hitler] does not think things out in a logical and consistent fashion, gathering all available information pertinent to the problem, mapping out alternative courses of action, and then weighing the evidence pro and con for each of them before reaching a decision. His mental processes operate in reverse. Instead of studying the problem as an intellectual would do, he avoids it and occupies himself with other things until unconscious processes furnish him with a solution. Having the solution, he then begins to look for facts that will prove it is correct. In this procedure he is very clever, and by the time he presents it to his associates, it has the appearance of a rational judgment. . . . His orientation is that of an artist and not that of a statesman."[13]

That approach would not have been nearly as effective had Hitler been without charisma. He had an exceptional ability to captivate, whether in individual meetings or in large groups. People who met him in small gatherings were often taken by the intensity of his blue-gray eyes or the strength of his guttural voice. At the massive Party rallies, his ability to shape and direct the mood of the audience was so powerful, ambulance crews were stationed to assist people who swooned.[14]

Behind the scenes, this personal appeal was enhanced by the youthfulness and generally low caliber of Hitler's associates. Most of his key department heads were in their thirties and all had - to use one's candid expression - a "flaw in the weave."[15] His second in command was a corrupt morphine addict, his propaganda minister an infatuated sycophant, his SS chief a former chicken rancher, his foreign minister a fool, his armaments minister an overly ambitious careerist, and his chancellery secretary a brutal and obsequious gatekeeper. With the sole exception of the armaments minister, these

---

[13] Walter C. Langer, *The Mind of Adolf Hitler* (New York: Basic Books, Inc. Publishers, 1972), p.74.
[14] Nick Clarke, *Alistair Cooke* (New York: Arcade Publishing, 1999), p.50.
[15] Speer, p.122.

were people whose only hope for status and wealth was pleasing Adolf Hitler. Not one of them was an independent personality.[16]

The dependency of Hitler's associates was deepened by their dislike for one another, a quality Hitler exacerbated by delegating overlapping administrative authority and starting turf wars. That strategy was intentional. Hitler the leader regularly subverted managerial efficiency in order to guarantee his own security. As a result, no single associate was ever strong enough to dream of challenging the Fuhrer - one word from Hitler and the others would have pounced - and any informal alliances were invariably short-lived.[17]

This calculated undermining of management was also achieved through compartmentalization of responsibilities. With the advent of the war, Hitler issued an order that, in the guise of protecting State secrets, established strict controls on the exchange of information.[18] Although the controls were harmful to the efficient conduct of the war effort, eventually they aided the implementation of the Holocaust. Civil servants and the military could avert their eyes from monstrous actions and pretend that they were not ethically responsible because they were not managerially responsible. Thus, people who scheduled trains for the death camps could see themselves as train schedulers and not accessories to mass murder because they were not to question where the trains went or what happened at the destination. If their involvement was more direct, they could insist that they were only following orders. [Satirist Tom Lehrer spoofed this attitude in a song skewering a German scientist's involvement in the rocket attacks on

---

[16] Dr. Louis Snyder, *Encyclopedia of the Third Reich* (New York: Paragon House, 1989). See individual entries.

[17] Norman Rich, *Hitler's War Aims: Ideology, the Nazi State and the Course of Expansion* (New York: W.W. Norton & Company, Inc., 1974), p.12; Speer, p.210; H.R. Trevor-Roper, *The Last Days of Hitler* (New York: The Macmillan Company, 1947), p.39.

[18] Gerald Fleming, *Hitler and The Final Solution* (Berkeley: University of California Press, 1984), pp.136-137; Edward N. Peterson, *The Limits of Hitler's Power* (Princeton: Princeton University Press, 1969), p.32.

London: "'Once the rockets are up, who cares where they come down? That's not my department,' says Wernher von Braun."[19]]

To complicate matters even further, the Fuhrerprinzip also accorded the force of supreme law to Hitler's every utterance. Hitler could either give the recipient of his remarks greater discretion and flexibility by issuing a vague form of command known as a Fuhrer Directive or bind them with a more specific Fuhrer Order that - theoretically - had to be carried out to the letter.[20]

In practice, Fuhrer Orders concealed far more than they restricted. Most were not written. They could range from the trivial to the most substantive, truly any subject Hitler chose to wheeze on about. Since their authority pre-empted all other laws and orders, they became the administrative equivalent of nitroglycerine. The unwritten ones could be used to implement insidious programs, such as the Holocaust, where the Fuhrer - like any gangland boss - sought deniability. It is revealing that although not one extermination order has surfaced with Hitler's signature, there is no doubt that he was the architect of what the Nazis, in characteristic bureaucratese, called the "final" or "total solution."[21]

Along with deniability, the use of verbal Fuhrer Orders created significant chaos because recipients could easily attach their own interpretations of Hitler's intent. Insiders such as Secretary to the Fuhrer Martin Bormann could announce the issuance of a Fuhrer Order and who was to say it was untrue? One result of this potential for abuse was a rush by Hitler's other top associates to place spies among the office personnel so the Fuhrer's true feelings could be transmitted without undue editing. Reports on Hitler's positions were especially helpful before any staff meetings so the associate could

---

[19] Tom Lehrer, *Too Many Songs* By Tom Lehrer (New York: Pantheon Books, 1981), p.154.

[20] Fleming, p.51.

[21] Richard Breitman, *The Architect of Genocide: Himmler and The Final Solution* (New York: Alfred A. Knopf, 1991), p.21 As SS Reichsfuhrer Heinrich Himmler explained to an audience of Wermacht officers, "When the Fuhrer gave me the order to carry out the total solution of the Jewish question, I at first hesitated, uncertain whether I could demand of my worthy SS men the execution of such a horrid assignment. . . . But this was ultimately a matter of a Fuhrer Order, and therefore I could have no misgivings." [Fleming, p.xxvii.]

arrive and then appear to independently voice the same opinion as the Fuhrer.[22]

Hitler appeared oblivious to his staff's machinations, choosing to focus his primary attention on the war effort where he committed the old autocratic sin of micro-management. Elsewhere, he delegated massive amounts of power and then ignored matters unless crisis forced him to address them. He didn't care if his associates acted foolishly or corruptly so long as they didn't interfere with his leadership goals. The thought that their mismanagement of the economy and other sectors might hamper or destroy the achievement of those same leadership goals does not appear to have occurred to him. This was, after all, the leader who decided to fight a war while dedicating precious resources to send millions of his country's most talented citizens to concentration camps.[23]

Such irrationality was possible because Hitler's charisma produced an autocracy that resembled a cult far more than it did a political movement. Charismatic executives in a normal enterprise might have considered the extent to which their charisma was debilitating to the independent judgment of their associates, but Hitler cared not a whit for any judgment other than his own. It is telling that even military officers who were not fanatical Nazis found that exposure to Hitler for extended periods of time could alter their judgment and render them increasingly dependent on his ideas and approval.[24]

Those in the inner circle, of course, were less able to break the spell. As years passed, their exposure to his charismatic aura created a psychiatric phenomenon called "folie a deux." Described as "the sharing of a delusional system by two or more individuals," folie a deux requires several ingredients. First, the charismatic leader attracts people with dependency needs, a prerequisite Hitler easily satisfied. If events cause the leader to become angry with his associates, he instead focuses his hostility on others, as when Hitler ranted against

---

[22] Speer, p.245.

[23] Ibid., p.294.

[24] Alan Bullock, *Hitler: A Study in Tyranny* (New York: Harper & Row, 1962), p.409.

the Jews, the Allies or the German General Staff. The leader then takes actions that are "delusionary" and the subordinates are faced with a terrible choice.[25] In business writer Manfred F. R. Kets de Vries' analysis:

> "If a subordinate resists, such leaders become overtly hostile, including them in their vision of 'the other camp' - the enemy. Naturally, the subordinate's level of anxiety rises. A double-bind situation develops for the subordinate; he or she has to choose between the loss of gratification of his or her dependency needs and exposure to the wrath of the leader, on the one hand, and the loss of reality, on the other."[26]

Hitler's associates chose to abandon reality. They believed in his ability to win the war even when he was directing military operations on a Berlin street map. As late as March 3, 1945, the top admiral of the German Navy would tell his commanders, "Let us place our trust unconditionally in Adolf Hitler's leadership. Believe me, in my two years as Navy Commander in Chief I have found that his strategic views always turn out right."[27] Since the Soviets overran Berlin and Hitler shot himself a little over a month after that remark, one can see just how deluded the Fuhrer's followers had become. The Fuhrer, of course, was the most deluded of all. Near the end, he looked back on his handiwork and reflected, "Afterwards, you rue the fact that you've been so kind."[28]

Autocratic executives who bolster their power with charisma carry an enormous potential for disaster. The greater their power, the more sweeping the appeal of their charisma. And the more sweeping that appeal, the greater the likelihood their staffs will join and encourage them in the creation of fantasy worlds. The appeal of their

---

[25] Manfred F.R. Kets DeVries, *Prisoners of Leadership* (New York: John Wiley & Sons, 1989), p.120 and p.124.

[26] Ibid., p.124.

[27] David Irving, *Hitler's War* (New York: The Viking Press, 1977), p.778 and p.783. I cite Irving only for the quotation and the related thoughts and not for any of his bizarre theories on the Holocaust.

[28] Paul Johnson, *Modern Times: The World from the Twenties to the Eighties* (New York: Harper & Row, 1983), p.413.

leadership weakens their management system which in time weakens their leadership.

Grand visions require periodic reality checks in order to keep the vision from deteriorating into fantasy. The autocratic style, because of its tendency to discourage challenge and dissent, avoids those checks and eventually suffers the consequences. All autocratic executives are vulnerable to that decline. All should have term limits, but the charismatic ones have a particular need for such controls.

MARGARET THATCHER AND THE REVOLT OF THE BLUE BUNNIES

Hitler's example, due to its extreme nature, illustrates the sharp edges of the autocratic style. Subtler problems can be discovered by studying an executive operating in a democratic, even collegial, system filled with restrictions upon the executive's power. The British political system, where the chief executive officer is required to face a public grilling by the opposition twice a week and where the CEO is simply regarded as the "first among equals," offers an excellent example of a person using an autocratic style in a non-autocratic environment: Margaret Thatcher.

By the time she reached its highest office, Margaret Thatcher had long demonstrated an impressive ability to navigate the cut-throat world of British politics. A maverick conservative who had challenged her party's smug orthodoxy, she was the first woman to become Prime Minister and it is likely that many of the less courageous but equally ambitious in her party never forgave her for that success. Those factors, combined with her advocacy of conviction as opposed to compromise politics, made her - to borrow a phrase easily applied to another outsider, Benjamin Disraeli - as conspicuous as a flamingo in a barnyard.[29]

One of the great unacknowledged aspects of Thatcher's leadership and management difficulties was the problem autocratic

---

[29] Disraeli, of course, was a master of compromise politics.

female executives can have when dealing with male associates. Whenever political commentators criticized "her autocratic style," it was often difficult to determine whether their problem was the "autocratic" aspect, "her" or a combination of the two. A reason for that suspicion is the sexism generally present in the British political scene. When Thatcher was a Cabinet minister, the opposition Laborites thought nothing of shouting "Ditch the Bitch" during her Parliamentary speeches.[30] Sexist jibes continued throughout her rise. The Labor Prime Minister once responded to her during the question period in Parliament with "Now, now little lady. You don't want to believe all those things you read in the newspapers. . . . Dearie me, not at all."[31] After she became prime minister, a prominent Labor Party leader taunted her male associates, saying they had been reduced to "neutered zombies"; an indication that they'd lost their manhood by working for an autocratic woman.[32] The nicknames given to her were equally revealing: Attila the Hen, Rambona, Rhoda the Rhino, The Great She-Elephant and Virago Intacta.[33] A few of her own Cabinet members privately referred to her as the "old bag" and "the old cow."[34] And Thatcher herself was not above dabbling in sexist banter when she analyzed her situation.

"In politics," she quipped, "if you want anything said, ask a man; if you want anything done, ask a woman."[35] There was more to that than a simple joke; it was the reaction of a talented woman who had spent years listening to powerful men pontificate while she had to prove herself by producing. Unfortunately, this frustration led to a forceful management style that could be unnecessarily abrasive. In her memoirs, Thatcher stated her defense by characteristically taking the offense: "My experience is that a group of men sitting around a table like little better than their own voices and that nothing is more

---

[30] Chris Ogden, *Maggie: An Intimate Portrait of a Woman in Power* (New York: Simon & Schuster, 1990), p.110.
[31] Ibid., p.140.
[32] Ibid., p.197.
[33] Denis Healey, *The Time of My Life* (London: Penguin Books, 1989), p.485.
[34] Alan Watkins, *A Conservative Coup: The Fall of Margaret Thatcher* (London: Duckworth, 1992), p.114.
[35] Ogden, p.102.

distasteful than the possibility that a conclusion can be reached without all of them having the chance to read from their briefs. My style of chairmanship certainly nonplussed some colleagues, who knew their brief a good deal less than I did."[36]

It is possible to acknowledge much truth in that observation and yet sense both a sexism spawned by bitterness and an eagerness to discount opposing opinions in the name of strong leadership. Even one of her supporters noted, "She's a woman in a man's world and is never entirely certain how to deal with men, so she flattens them."[37] On occasion, that practice could cause her to "out macho" her male colleagues and take harsher action than a man would have taken under similar circumstances.

But not always. Although her autocratic style could both confront and console, all in the tradition of the benevolent padrone, there also was a certain sexual electricity to Thatcher's relationship with her associates. She referred to the blue-suited men in her governing circle as her "blue bunnies," she was not adverse to considering good looks when reviewing a candidate's qualifications for a job and flirting was not an unknown part of her arsenal.[38]

Thatcher may not have been "entirely certain how to deal with men," but she knew enough of human nature to know that sending mixed signals can be a way of throwing your associates - and any potential adversary - off balance. Besides, matters were relative: the blue bunnies were even more baffled by the presence of a strong woman in the prime ministership, one who could alternatively charm and command.

Male-female dynamics not only surfaced when some minister didn't know his brief as well as the prime minister, they also went to the heart of Thatcher's leadership-management style. Her chief

[36] Margaret Thatcher, *The Downing Street Years* (New York: Harper Collins, 1993), p.561.
[37] Ogden, p.304.
[38] Anthony Sampson, *The Changing Anatomy of Britain* (New York: Random House, 1982), p.46; Ogden, p.204. This odd combination of sexuality and assertiveness was noted by French President Francois Mitterand who described Thatcher as possessing "The eyes of Caligula but the mouth of Marilyn Monroe." One suspects that Mitterand fantasized a bit during those London-Paris summits.

advantage as a leader was that she knew precisely what she wanted to do. Her chief disadvantage as a manager was that, after years of governing well, she reached a point where she believed that she could neglect important management tasks, such as ensuring the commitment of her team, and not pay a price. She underestimated the extent to which her autocratic management style could create managerial problems that could lash back and derail her leadership strategy.[39]

She forgot she was acting autocratically in a non-autocratic system, one that stressed the value of collective decision making. She wanted to act as a president while a number of her Cabinet ministers wanted her to act as simply as a first among equals, sort of a Prime Facilitator. She disdained such attempts to make her, as she saw it, lead from a crowd. Despite her efforts to strengthen her own decision making authority by reducing the influence of the Cabinet, the system remained and, as executives can discover to their delight or dismay, the system can be a weapon.[40]

Rather than confronting the traditional system - or myth - of collective responsibility and formally changing the role of the prime minister, Thatcher chose to alter it informally. Her preferred method for dealing with internal opponents - flattened or not - was to circumvent them. Increasingly, she used an inner circle of true believers that was smaller than her formal Cabinet and less likely to leak potential projects to the press. This functioned well for a while but, as time passed, it became too clever by half.[41]

The old clash between leadership and management began to surface. Those who had to implement various programs started to resent their exclusion from the inner circle that decided the direction of those programs. Foreign Secretary Geoffrey Howe objected to the influence of foreign affairs advisor Charles Powell. Chancellor of the

---

[39] Thatcher, p.755.
[40] Watkins, p.48.
[41] Ogden, pp.143-144, 250, 304; Nigel Lawson, *The View From No.11: Memoirs of a Tory Radical* (London: Corgi Books, 1992), p.127; Hennessy, pp.100-102; John Ranelagh, *Thatcher's People: An insider's account of the politics, the power and the personalities* (London: Fontana, 1991), p.303.

Exchequer Nigel Lawson had an even stronger concern about the Prime Minister's ties to economic advisor Alan Walters.[42]

Thatcher's autocratic style, which was far from soothing to bruised egos, exacerbated these hurt feelings. It was not just the "wets" - those members of the Conservative Party's moderate liberal faction - who were upset with her. Prominent "drys" - advocates of Thatcher's own free market and firm anti-Communist policies - also began to bridle at her methods. Her associates had once humorously shortened one of her favorite phrases - "There is no alternative" - to TINA. But the passage of time and the wounding of feelings made what had been strength appear to be arbitrariness. The autocracy was becoming a form of negative social alchemy: people who had been friends were turning into adversaries, even enemies.[43]

The irony is that the Iron Lady, the woman who broke the power of the miners' union, lectured the Soviet leaders, humbled the Argentine dictators during the Falklands War and regularly flummoxed the Labor Party leaders in the House of Commons, would be insufficiently autocratic when it came to a crucial management moment. That event was lurking in Thatcher's future, waiting in ambush, and when it pounced her leadership concerns would blur her management vision. The Iron Lady would fail to act decisively and all would be lost.

To understand Margaret Thatcher's fall we must consider her surroundings. Her leadership-management problems were worsened by a political system that requires that all Cabinet members - including the prime minister - be members of Parliament, the British equivalent of Congress. Most are members of the House of Commons, which holds the real legislative power, although traditionally there is some token representation from the advisory House of Lords. In most instances, if a Cabinet member is sacked by the Prime Minister, rather than going off into the political wilderness, he or she simply returns to the House of Commons and sits on what are quaintly called the back benches, the section reserved for members who do not hold ministerial office. Because the longevity of

---

[42] Lawson, pp.431, 961, 971; Ranelagh, p.281.
[43] Ogden, pp.131, 143-144; Ranelagh, pp.284.

any prime minister - indeed any political party's time in power - depends on the ability to win votes of confidence in Parliament, if the Prime Minister fires too many Cabinet ministers, or fails to reward enough of the ambitious, a large faction of grumblers may accumulate on the back benches, people who either resent a dismissal or who believe they should have been appointed to higher office. A few, it can be expected, even lust for the prime minister's job. Since there are no term limits, a successful prime minister can, in Thatcher's phrase, go on and on and on. The catch is the longer the prime ministership, the greater the number of malcontents within the prime minister's own party.[44]

Why is this significant? Because prime ministers can be challenged in a leadership election where the party's members of Parliament, including all those disgruntled back benchers, can vote. If a sufficient majority is not won, the prime minister is jettisoned.[45]

Margaret Thatcher's success caused her to serve longer than any Prime Minster in this century. As the years passed, she fired a bundle of ministers and they dutifully trudged off to work, vegetate, plot and/or heckle from the back benches. She possessed the wit to give many of those exiles a peerage and dispatch them to Britain's elegant Siberia, the House of Lords, where they could cause less trouble. But a sizable bloc longed for the day when they could, in the name of Queen and country, put a knife in their leader.[46] Unknown to most of them, their opportunity began in July 1989. For on the morning Prime Minister Thatcher was to depart for the European Summit in Madrid, two of her senior blue bunnies decided to bare their teeth.

Foreign Secretary Geoffrey Howe and Chancellor of the Exchequer Nigel Lawson, both of them long-time Thatcherites who had become alienated by her policies and her style, told the Prime Minister they wanted Britain to join the Exchange Rate Mechanism (ERM) for European currencies. Their opinion on ERM was no surprise to Thatcher; she'd heard and rejected their arguments in the

---

[44] Bill Jones, ed., *Politics UK* (London: Philip Allen, 1991), pp.386-411.
[45] Ibid., p.403.
[46] Ogden, p.313.

past. Their new position, however, was a stunner: If she did not agree to their recommendation, they would resign.[47]

Thatcher, unwisely as it turned out, blinked. Fearing that to lose such key ministers on the eve of a European summit would invite disaster, she instead gave them a compromise course of action that outlined some vague conditions for British ERM membership, but in truth gave them little at all for the Prime Minister retained the power to determine when those conditions were met.[48]

Despite their threats, the two rebels continued to serve in Thatcher's Cabinet.

Later, as dispute over policy worsened, Nigel Lawson resigned because of his continuing disapproval of Thatcher's use of economic advisor Alan Walters. Thatcher later moved Geoffrey Howe to another post and he too eventually resigned, making an extraordinary farewell speech in the House of Commons in which he castigated the Prime Minister. This, coupled with Thatcher's low standing in the public opinion polls due to an ill-chosen battle over a poll tax, triggered a leadership challenge from still another former Cabinet minister - Michael Heseltine - who had long coveted the job of prime minister.[49]

In the leadership election, a mere four votes kept Margaret Thatcher from achieving a sufficient majority to keep the challenge from going on to a second ballot. It was a thin but lethal margin. Recognizing that her power was irretrievably weakened, she resigned.[50]

It is easy to conclude that Thatcher could have used some advice from Thrasybulus on how to deal with potential opponents but is it entirely fair? The British Prime Minister was in the classic bind faced by many female executives who have to operate in a predominantly male environment: if you act assertively or autocratically, you risk being labeled a bitch and if you act unassertively, you risk being steamrollered by male associates who see kindness and

---

[47] Thatcher, p.712.
[48] Ibid., pp.712-713; Watkins, p.119.
[49] Thatcher, pp.713-718, 757, 839-842.
[50] Ibid., pp.844, 856-857.

accommodation as signs of weakness. This either-or choice causes many women to choose the former because it is better to be maligned than destroyed. The choice, however, is a false one.

A woman can use an autocratic style without evoking immediate cries of bitchiness if she distinguishes between the petty and the important. Not every battle has to be won. Not every error has to be corrected. Only the important ones need be. Rather than showing up some minister who did not prepare properly for a cabinet meeting and thereby gaining that minister's antipathy, Thatcher would have been better advised to draw careful boundaries and let her Cabinet colleagues know if they crossed into the danger zone. Whenever anyone violated those guidelines, she should have acted firmly and fairly.

British political writer John Ranelagh concluded that Thatcher "did not have the male attitude to conflict; there is a sticking point beyond which men will not normally go, largely because they realize that to go further means fighting to the death."[51] Margaret Thatcher often went past that point but, due to her sex, her actions provoked conspiracy rather than open combat.

There is evidence Thatcher was hurt by the criticism of her style and consequently altered her actions to avoid expanding her "Bossy Boots" image. If so, she should have adjusted in the trivial areas rather than an essential one. Howe and Lawson went well beyond the line of professional propriety. The Prime Minister should have accepted their resignations or sacked them. The timing of their demand was an indefensible administrative ambush and would have been seen as such by the public. Better to exile such adversaries to the back benches than keep them within a sword's length in the Cabinet.

Had she earlier adopted a less abrasive but nonetheless firm approach, it is unlikely that her dissenting Cabinet colleagues would have felt ill-used enough or bold enough to launch an open break. Geoffrey Howe, whose speech helped sink Thatcher, was an ideological soul mate who had served with her from the start. He was hardly known for his ferocity; in fact, a Labor Party opponent had once described an attack by Howe as "rather like being savaged by a dead sheep." But Thatcher had pushed a gentle man too far; so far that he was able to disguise treachery under the noble title of self-defense.[52]

Like many autocrats, Thatcher never acknowledged the root cause of her difficulties. Even with the added advantage of hindsight, she would use a leader's lenses to analyze what was a managerial problem:

"I was . . . wrong on one important matter. Of course, I understand that some of my Cabinet colleagues and other ministers were more to the left, some more to the right. But I believed that they had generally become convinced of the rightness of the basic principles as I had. Orthodox finance, low levels of regulation and taxation, a minimal bureaucracy, strong defense, a willingness to stand up for British interests wherever and whenever threatened - I did not believe that I had to open windows into men's souls on these matters. The arguments for them seemed to me to have been won. I now know that such arguments are never finally won."[53]

Thatcher's analysis misses the managerial dimension, the fact that differences over issues became secondary to the way in which she treated people. As a stereotypic autocratic boss, she was dismissing the complaints of subordinates as the grumbles of people who lacked fiber or commitment when in many cases their complaints were generated by a lack of respect. She did not fall because of some grand ideological division, however much both sides would like to portray it as such. She fell because she neglected the managerial task of team building.

Was Thatcher a failure? Absolutely not when one considers her early years in office. Due to her extraordinary abilities, Margaret Thatcher on a bad day was better than many of her opponents were on their good ones. But as time passed the corrosive nature of her autocratic style continued to wear away her effectiveness and the British political system, with its preference for the collegial over the autocratic, eventually pulled her down. Had she learned to

---

[51] Ranalagh, pp.27-28.
[52] Ogden, p.319.
[53] Thatcher, p.755.

compensate for the negative aspects of her management style, she could have lasted longer but she would not have been able to maintain the brilliance of her earlier years.

Corporate executives and managers have fewer restraints than prime ministers and so may more easily elude the misfortune of being given their walking papers. Unfortunately, this job security encourages illogical thinking. "If I'm here and things are going reasonably well," they reason, "then I'm a success." Such questionable logic ignores the autocrat's impact on the effectiveness of the organization and fails to place that effectiveness against an objective benchmark. For if an executive causes the organization to operate at a B level when it could be operating at an A, how can that be called success?

CHURCHILL'S SEARING SEARCHLIGHT

No autocrat ever had more cause to exceed the boundaries of law, management and civility than Winston Churchill. When Churchill was named prime minister, Britain needed leadership far more than it needed management. His predecessor, the gray and stolid Neville Chamberlain, was a good manager who'd taken his country right into the jaws of a beast. By the time Churchill entered No.10 Downing Street, German troops were in the midst of their blitzkrieg through Belgium, the Netherlands, Luxembourg and France. The British war effort was in a state of disarray and if France fell, Britain was an obvious target for invasion. It was the sort of crisis in which autocrats are most effective.

On the surface, Churchill and Thatcher were quite similar. Churchill, however, didn't face ingrained sexism and he was able to cultivate a curmudgeonly charm. Sir George Mallarby, Undersecretary in the Cabinet Office, commented on the Churchill magic:

> "Anybody who served anywhere near him was devoted to him. It is hard to say why. He was not kind or considerate. He bothered

nothing about us. He knew the names only of those very close to him and would hardly let anyone else come into his presence. He was free with abuse and complaint. He was exacting beyond reason and ruthlessly critical. He continuously exhibited all the characteristics that one morally deplores and abominates in the boss. Not only did he get away with it but nobody really wanted him otherwise. He was unusual, unpredictable, exciting, original, stimulating, provocative, outrageous, uniquely experienced, abundantly talented, humorous, entertaining - almost everything a man could be, a great man."[54]

Churchill's greatest advantage was that he had the excuse of a crisis. With the Nazis just across the English Channel, actions that would never have been forgiven in peacetime became bold strokes or were excused as the inevitable by-products of a man under stress. Moreover, after the passivity of the Chamberlain years, the government was ready for an aggressive leader, which was a role Churchill was more than willing to fill.

Having been bitten by some decisions during the First World War, Churchill was alert to the machinations of organizations. It is revealing that while one of Hitler's first acts at the onset of war was to carefully compartmentalize information so decisions could be hidden and responsibility evaded, Churchill sought to preserve communication so responsibility could be clarified. Churchill's order perfectly fit his demeanor, his powerful writing abilities and his work schedule:

"Let it be very clearly understood that all directions emanating from me are made in writing, or should be immediately afterwards confirmed in writing, and that I do not accept any responsibility for matters relating to national defense on which I am alleged to have given decisions unless they are recorded in writing."[55]

Having matters reduced to writing may seem natural to a man who'd made his living as an author, but Churchill accomplished

---

[54] William Douglas Home, *The Prime Ministers* (New York: Barnes & Noble Books, 1987), pp.228-229.
[55] Sir John Wheeler-Bennett, ed., *Action This Day: Working With Churchill* (New York: St. Martin's Press, 1968), p.20.

several things with that directive. He set the standard as to how directions would be communicated, he protected himself against people who might want to put words in his mouth and he chose a communication medium that he handled very well and that could be accomplished at all hours.

It wasn't long after that directive that Churchill unleashed a continuous barrage of memos and dispatches designed to shake and stimulate the British war effort. Urgent messages went out with red labels ordering ACTION THIS DAY and officials throughout the government and military began to feel the broad extent of the new Prime Minister's interest and command. In June 1940 alone, these were some of the questions:

> "What progress is being made with rockets and sensitive fuses, with automatic bomb sights and radio direction finding? Can the Navy transfer pilots to Fighter Command? Can Turin and Milan be bombed? What about more felling of timber to reduce imports and save shipping? Can't more regular troops be brought from India, and a better reserve be built up in the Middle East? Who is responsible for making the 'sticky' bomb? 'Any chortling by officials who have been slothful in pushing this bomb over the fact that at present it has not succeeded will be viewed with great disfavor by me.' What is happening about the repatriation of evacuated French forces? And their wounded? Why can't civilians be employed on defense works to release more troops for active defense?"[56]

One official likened Churchill's queries to the beam of a searchlight "ceaselessly swinging round and penetrating into the remote recesses of the administration so that everyone, however humble his range or his function, felt that one day the beam might rest on him and light up what he was doing." The result of this was, the official noted, "a new sense of purpose and urgency.... as it came to

---

[56] Ronald Lewin, *Churchill As Warlord* (New York: Stein & Day, 1973), p.41. When Churchill served as prime minister in the 1950's, the office keeper located some ACTION THIS DAY labels, which had been preserved in case Churchill returned to power, and placed them on his desk. The time had come, however, to sacrifice bold leadership for calmer management. He never used them. See Wheeler-Bennett, pp.119-120.

be realized that a firm hand, guided by a strong will, was on the wheel."[57]

There is little doubt that Churchill's messages were often disruptive to management. He did not hesitate to venture into trivia, such as how to protect the animals in the London zoo, nor did he avoid sarcasm. He once reminded the First Sea Lord that warships are meant to go under fire and, in a note to the Chief Marshal for Air, noted, "I'm glad you have the matter, as you say, under examination. Pray report to me tomorrow what is going to be done."[58]

There was, however, a calculated limit to Churchill's autocracy. Although he argued ceaselessly with his military advisors - if they said an attack would not take place for 24 hours, they had to be prepared to justify how each hour of delay would be spent - he never overruled them when they presented a united front. His extraordinary experience in military affairs had acquainted him with the types of catastrophe that can result from poor planning, but it also taught him a healthy respect for the depth of knowledge held by such professionals as Montgomery and Brooke. He knew when to back off.[59]

One senses an important difference in the manner in which Churchill and Thatcher dealt with their associates. At one point Clement Attlee, the Labor Party leader who headed Britain's domestic efforts as part of a coalition cabinet, complained in a letter to Churchill that the Prime Minister was showing "very scant respect" for the views of his colleagues on domestic matters by failing to read briefing papers, second-guessing, digressing onto other topics and generally wasting their time at meetings. Furious, Churchill consulted some other advisors as well as his wife. They all replied that Attlee was right. A chastened Churchill wrote an apologetic letter to Attlee and promised to mend his ways.[60]

That episode shows a level of trust that was missing in the conflicts between Thatcher and her associates. The disgruntled men

---

[57] Ibid., p.22.
[58] Ibid., p.50; John Keegan, ed., *Churchill's Generals* (New York: Grove Weidenfeld, 1991), p.91; James Nelson, ed., *General Eisenhower on the Military Churchill* (New York: W.W. Norton & Company, Inc., 1970), p.28.
[59] Wheeler-Bennett, p.27.
[60] Kenneth Harris, *Attlee* (London: Weidenfeld and Nicolson, 1983), pp.241-244.

around Margaret Thatcher confronted her with a threat to resign; something Attlee would never have done. Churchill had a better relationship with the leading members of the opposition party than Thatcher had with some key members of her own party.

AUTOCRATIC LESSONS LEARNED

Autocrats are not noted for introspection. Corporate CEOs who terrorize their staffs eventually write cozy memoirs recounting the good old days and how all they'd wanted was a tight and happy ship. Newspaper magnate Robert Maxwell, who could "charm the birds off the trees and then shoot them," frequently mused that people should practice "The three Cs - consideration, concentration and conciseness."[61] Nice sentiments to be sure, but there is little evidence Maxwell himself embraced any of those qualities. While ITT's CEO, Harold Geneen held tension-filled annual Business Plan Review meetings that one of his former vice presidents likened to "The Caine Mutiny court martial scene with Queeg on the wrong side of the green cloth."[62] Geneen later went through the usual belated conversion, writing a business book where he gave sound and sensitive advice on how one should manage. It differed a bit from how Geneen actually managed.[63]

What the autocrats fail to realize is the extent to which they - the self-proclaimed defenders of no-nonsense performance - can be the problem. Given time, autocrats become the bull and the organization is their china closet. As their poor managerial practices achieve critical mass, these self-proclaimed yet dysfunctional defenders of excellence hamper and often block leadership goals. Autocratic executives spawn a series of dangerous management developments. Among them are:

---

[61] Tom Bower, *Maxwell: The Outsider* (London: Mandarin, 1988), pp.115 and 511.
[62] Burns, p.144.
[63] Harold Geneen with Alvin Moscow, *Managing* (New York: Avon, 1984).

Defective Decision Making

With the autocrat's habit of rewarding concurrence and punishing dissent, it doesn't take associates long to learn that the safest course is to give the autocrat whatever he or she wants, regardless of its negative impact on the organization.

In cases where the staff is completely intimidated by the autocrat, a variation of the Stockholm Syndrome may occur as the "hostages" begin to identify with their "captor." When dangling job security or status before desperate associates, the tyrannical boss finds more people seeking to ingratiate themselves than trying to flee. Rather than admitting weakness, those associates construct elaborate face-saving stories to excuse the tyrant's behavior or to justify their tolerance of it. Many try to reduce conflict by doctoring reports, fiddling with figures and cooking up new ways to demonstrate their loyalty.

Autocratic management encourages the development of "groupthink;" Irving Janus' term for decision making circles where dissenters withhold their opinions in order to be accepted by the group.[64] Chester Cooper, the White House Advisor for Asian Affairs in the Johnson administration, recalled how Lyndon Johnson would announce his decision on Vietnam policy and then ask for input from the National Security Council members, their assistants and members of the White House and NSC staffs. Cooper would imagine himself standing and declaring "Mr. President, gentlemen, I most definitely do **not** agree" only to hear himself called upon and replying, "Yes, Mr. President, I agree."[65] An elementary rule for all executives - and especially for the autocratic ones - is never to state your preference before obtaining the opinions of your staff. Autocrats who are genuinely interested in preventing group think should routinely appoint a "devil's advocate" - a staff member who is specifically designated to poke holes in the likely decision. [That role should be rotated and the devil's advocate must not be punished or ostracized.]

---

[64] Irving L. Janus, *Groupthink* (Boston: Houghton Mifflin Company, 1982).
[65] Chester L. Cooper, *The Lost Crusade: America in Vietnam* (New York: Dodd, Mead & Company, 1970), p.223.

Another helpful technique is "reverse decision-making" where the decision making group is asked to list ways in which blunders could be committed. The open discussion of dissenting or negative points often ferrets out any reservations held by a group member.

Acquiescence by Appointment

Autocrats who fire dissenters may be seeking "acquiescence by appointment." The German generals who were appointed by Hitler to replace those who had displeased him fell victim to this practice. Military historian Liddell Hart described the phenomenon: "A newly promoted general is always confident that the situation is better than it appeared to his predecessor, and that he can succeed where the latter failed. Such a disposition is a powerful lever in the hands of any ruler."[66]

Acquiescence by appointment feeds the autocrat's suspicion that those who dissent aren't disagreeing because of substantive reasons, but are doing so simply because of arbitrariness or a lack of will power. If a willing - and especially a well regarded - replacement can be found, the autocrat concludes the predecessor was a wimp or a nay-sayer.

This practice also creates a climate that favors unethical behavior. Once employees realize that being the bearer of bad news is terminal, they will go to great lengths to cover up or disguise the existence of problems.

Upward Delegation

The culture of dependency fostered by the autocrat encourages subordinates to push decisions up the ladder rather than resolve matters at the lowest possible level. When their associates act as if such low-grade items require the autocrat's attention, this feeds the autocrat's perception that matters cannot be delegated downward. The

---

[66] B.H. Liddell Hart, *The German Generals Talk* (New York: Quill, 1979), p.19.

upward delegation gobbles up the autocrat's schedule and steals time from more worthy projects. It also can be a tool of conniving associates who purposely besiege the autocrat with mundane matters in order to distract attention from subjects of potential embarrassment.

Very little can be done to discourage upward delegation if the executive continues to be an autocrat. To decentralize is to remove the controlling nature and the security-orientation of the autocrat. To recognize the restraints of a system is to shift from being an autocrat to being a formalistic executive.

Insensitivity to Others

The atmosphere of autocracy favors quick readings, simple explanations and obedience over extended debate. The autocrat's raison d'etre is action, not analysis, and so such prejudice is not surprising. Experts are often viewed with suspicion since their grasp of information makes them an intellectual rival to the autocrat. As a result, the organization develops a number of blind spots, especially in subjects requiring a human dimension. Insensitivity to others - a hallmark of the autocratic style - produces an inability to read actions that go beyond self-interest, that are buoyed by feelings.

Several years ago, the CEO of a major airline had a blind spot when dealing with his airline pilots. He wanted them to act in accordance with *his* logic, not theirs, and discounted the extent to which distrust and dislike of him would cause them to support a mechanics' strike. His autocratic style not only created hurt feelings and diminished respect, it also caused him to underestimate the impact of such intangibles. Once again, management style subverted a leadership aim.

The autocrat is often so focused on the bottom line that he or she does not appreciate that people will choose to ignore the bottom line if other important factors, such as self-respect and status, are not addressed. The leadership goals set by the autocrat can thus be affected - and subverted - by the attitudes engendered by the autocrat's routine management style.

Chaotic Succession

Autocratic management teams often are composed of people who have either repressed their misgivings in order to accommodate the autocrat or have willingly joined in the autocrat's vision. Independent thinkers who lack the desire or ability to bend departed earlier. It may not be impossible to find a strong leader in the ranks of the remaining associates, but it won't be as easy as it is in organizations where the CEO's style is more supportive of associate development.

The autocrat who cares for the future health of the organization will establish a term limit and stick to it. This lets the independent thinkers know that they'll eventually have a shot at either the top job or a different environment and that the autocrat is only there to correct a specific problem. Once the term limit is reached, the autocrat - regardless of how many other problems have arisen - must leave for the good of the organization. This automatic departure is important because autocrats can always find excuses to remain. If they remain, they will damage the organization.

Chapter 3

THE COLLEGIAL EXECUTIVE

In today's egalitarian workplace, where managers scurry to workshops on team-building or bond during company-sponsored river rafting expeditions, even the most resolute autocrat professes to be a collegial manager. Being collegial is "in." It fits neatly with the trends of empowerment and decentralization and the modern emphasis on being a "people person."

And its dangers are well-hidden.

At first glance, you wouldn't think collegial management could hold any threats. The term itself conjures visions of a happy band of equals sitting around a table, talking out the problems of the day: An inclusive, dynamic bunch, all committed - in their intellectually diverse ways - to the same central mission.

It doesn't work out that way. Unless precautions are taken, the management problems inherent in the collegial style begin to subvert the leadership goals.

Unlike the autocratic style, where the executive risks the drawbacks of dictatorship, and the formalistic style, where the executive makes decisions based upon information that has been carefully coordinated - and often carefully filtered - by the staff, the collegial management style seeks a frank exchange between the primary decision maker and a select group of advisors. Those advisors may come from any level of the organization and may vary from topic to topic, for this dynamic approach doesn't truck with hierarchy and pulling rank. This is the style of today's energetic executive, the savvy facilitator, who possesses the ability to exist at the swirling center of this thought vortex, probing the reasoning of the associates, sucking up information and synthesizing the hodgepodge of ideas into workable policy.

Or so it seems.

In practice, the collegial style can result in the executive being less informed, less in control and more prone to mistakes, be they managerial or ethical. As we shall see, even agile minds can be trapped by this seductive style for, like many vices, its dangers lie hidden beneath the folds of its virtues.

In general, the collegial style of management presents these obstacles:

The collegial style requires exceptional facilitating and diplomatic skills by the leader-manager. Consider the demands of the collegial style. Rather than relying upon a bureaucracy to filter the information, the collegial executive assembles ad hoc teams that cross organizational lines of authority and dip into, sometimes far into, the depths of the organization. This information gathering may be done via formal meetings. It may also be accomplished informally, such as when the executive directly calls the first line supervisor rather than talking to her boss. Either way, it places the information-giver on the spot. He or she has to respond directly to the boss's boss or sometimes even the boss's boss's boss, and hope that candor does not inadvertently make policy or embarrass a supervisor. These "info raids" and the inevitable "Let me tell you what I just told your supervisor" phone calls can be highly disruptive to the organization and erode the status of those supervisors who have been by-passed in this reverse "bungee" version of jumping the chain of command.

The collegial executive has to be able to perform such raids without creating undue disruption or animosity because the unspoken message of such contacts is that truth is not always available through normal channels. That unspoken message should be carefully considered. When collegials talk about cutting through the bureaucracy, they are talking about their own organizations. When they continually use end-runs, expedited procedures and special advisors, they are announcing that they lack either the will or the ability to correct their own organization.

Extraordinary interpersonal skills must be used by the executive if he or she facilitates these information gathering sessions. The ability to draw out the reluctant, control the domineering and protect the dissenter while keeping the team from breaking apart is no small challenge. Many executives lacking the patience and necessary social skills, find themselves dabbling in the collegial, creating chaos and then quickly pulling rank in order to restore order.

Furthermore, as organizations become more diverse, with greater numbers of women and minorities involved in major decisions, the collegial style will require more sophisticated communication skills than those in the days when the only faces around the conference table were those of white males. Executives using this style will have to be able to pick up on the subtle signals of each participant, rather than assuming that every one is from the same culture and using the same communication rule book.

Not all cultures appreciate the free-wheeling nature of the collegial. Some prefer the clarity of hierarchy and are at sea when tossed into a collegial environment. Others may resist the high speed at which collegial systems operate and instead favor a more methodical system - such as the formalistic - where authority receives greater deference and where brainstorming is less spontaneous. For example, in one major corporation where the virtues of collegiality were unquestioned, some professionals who had recently immigrated from Asia sat silent during staff meetings. The impromptu and fast-paced brainstorming sessions made them uncomfortable because they felt opinions should not be surfaced without some preparation. Once this problem was recognized, the organization began to circulate agenda sheets in advance of the meetings. The agenda sheets specified the topics to be discussed, the reluctant brainstormers could then prepare their contributions and their participation rate began to climb.

The collegial style requires a great deal of time and energy. A central aspect of the collegial approach is its fear that information will be filtered or distorted. Consequently, the executive becomes the hub and the associates become the spokes. This ensures that the executive knows more than everyone else, but it also means he or she has to devote time and energy to ferreting out that information. Even the most vigorous executive risks exhaustion and an ultimate decline in effectiveness. What was a stellar decision making process three months ago may be haphazard today because the collegial executive is simply worn out.

The collegial discourages delegation. Since the collegial executive is the central clearing house for information and since much of the information is obtained through meetings and informal discussion, it becomes extremely time-consuming for the executive to transfer that information to a subordinate. Rather than handing over a staff or briefing paper, the executive would have to give a lengthy explanation of all of the various aspects of the subject. Usually, the amount of time for such activity is prohibitive, so no delegation occurs. As a result, the collegial system extracts even more time from the executive's schedule. It also weakens the capabilities of the associates since they do not have access to an institutional memory preserved in memos or minutes; the rationale for significant decisions is stored in the executive's head.

The collegial encourages short-term thinking. The collegial's bureaucracy-busting ways promise speed and speed is not always a virtue. Rather than waiting on the decisions to bubble up through the organization's staffing process, the collegial assembles a group of advisors, conducts an accelerated analysis, and reaches a decision. The focus is on what is doable, not what is best, and collegials often describe themselves as pragmatists. A danger of this process is short-term thinking. Because of the transitory nature of the collegial group and the emphasis on speed and pragmatism, long-term interests may be ignored or downplayed.

The collegial style can be manipulated by the executive. The economist Paul Samuelson once remarked, "He who picks his own doctor from an array of competing doctors is in a real sense his own doctor."[67] So it is with the collegial executive who, while pretending to elicit a broad range of opinion, selects those advisors who are likely to offer agreement or praise. The process only works if genuine, articulate dissenters are encouraged to present their views.

The collegial style can inadvertently encourage hubris. Although the collegial style purports to be egalitarian, closer examination reveals that its pragmatism can encourage a dangerous propensity for arrogance. All organizations risk abuses by the inner circle. The collegial executive and his or her team, however, must be on special guard. Their style purports to include outside or dissenting opinion, but often only reflects carefully chosen opinion. Furthermore, by emphasizing pragmatism over principles they may give excessive weight to the bottom line and encourage ethical lapses. When these circumstances arise, true collegiality is replaced by false collegiality, where the executive manipulates certain results by choosing procedures or team members who are likely to produce such results. Anyone who has seen resolutions railroaded past a Parent Teacher Association meeting or a church executive committee has likely witnessed false collegiality in action.

This fall from grace should not be surprising. The pragmatist, in the end, is contemptuous of ideologies, procedures, regulations and platforms because those are restraints on his or her ability to act. Collegial executives who are enamored with pragmatism want the maximum capability to make decisions on their terms. They want an ideology of pragmatism because they, as the decision makers, are its high priests, the sole determiners of what is and is not pragmatic. Their close associates are the aristocracy. Pragmatism, to paraphrase Dr. Johnson, can be the last refuge of many a scoundrel.

The collegial cloaks, but doesn't eliminate, office politics. Just as the collegial executive can manipulate, so too can that executive be manipulated. The collegial executive who believes that the inclusive process prevents office politics is naive. Coalitions will form outside of the formal structures. Indeed, because formal status is devalued in the collegial process and access to the executive is possible for lower

---

[67] Henry Fairlie, *The Kennedy Promise* (New York: Dell Publishing Co., Inc., 1973), p.124.

level officials, gaining access to the top decision maker can become a preoccupation for the power-hungry. Former White House Press Secretary George Reedy once said, in reference to the ultra-ambitious, amoral climber in Budd Schulberg's novel *What Makes Sammy Run?*, "The life of a courtier is to be Sammy Glick or to fight Sammy Glick."[68] The collegial system does not automatically bar the Sammy Glicks of the world. It may, due to its expanded opportunities for access to the top decision maker and favor dispenser, actually increase their numbers.

JOHN F. KENNEDY'S COLLEGIALLY-PRODUCED QUAGMIRE

The collegial management style attained prominence during John F. Kennedy's administration as part of the ultra-cool, buttoned-down image of Camelot. Kennedy and the ambitious young executives and idealists who clustered about his version of The Round Table didn't want an autocrat-dominated corps of dependents nor did they seek to replicate what was seen as the stuffy and bureaucratic formalism of the Eisenhower years.[69] Collegial management proclaimed both a new style and a new leader; a prince who listened to a cadre composed of so-called Irish mafia politicos and action intellectuals and whose mental acuity, determination and energy could humble any management problem. Historian James MacGregor Burns mocked the press descriptions of the new leader and his management technique:

> "He [JFK] is not only the handsomest, the best dressed, the most articulate, and graceful as a gazelle. He is omniscient; he swallows and digests whole books in minutes; his eye seizes instantly on the

---

[68] Charles Peters and Nicholas Lemann, ed., *Inside the System* (New York: Holt, Rinehart and Winston, 1979), p.36. (Article by Russell Baker and Charles Peters entitled "The Prince and His Courtiers: At the White House, the Kremlin, and the Reichchancellery").

[69] Richard Tanner Johnson, *Managing The White House: An Intimate Study of the Presidency* (New York: Harper & Row, Publishers, 1974), pp.124-125. In this pioneering work, Johnson uses competitive, formalistic and collegial to distinguish presidential management styles from Franklin Roosevelt through Richard Nixon.

crucial point of a long memorandum; he confounds experts with superior knowledge of their field. He is omnipresent; no sleepy staff member can be sure that he will not telephone - or pop in; every hostess at a party can hope that he will. He is omnipotent; he personally bosses and spurs the whole shop; he has no need of Ike's staff apparatus; he is more than a lion, more than a fox. He's Superman!"[70]

Burns was cleverly alluding to his own biography of Franklin Delano Roosevelt in which he referred to FDR as the lion and the fox. Whenever Kennedy charted his administration, the ghost of FDR, the man who had shaped the modern presidency, was in the room. Like JFK, Franklin D. Roosevelt also wanted to be at the center of things, but he wasn't into collegial management; he preferred raw manipulation.

"There is something to be said for having a little conflict," Roosevelt said. "'A little rivalry is stimulating, you know. It keeps everyone going to prove he is a better fellow than the next man. It keeps them honest too."[71]

Roosevelt didn't just tolerate rivalry. He created it by playing staff members off against one another and giving associates overlapping assignments and then watching as they punched it out. His Cabinet often resembled an assembly of bitter enemies, but FDR didn't care because he believed that their rivalry kept him better informed. He sat at the center and manipulated them all with a combination of charm and ruthlessness.[72] War Secretary Henry Stimson fumed, "He has never been a good administrator and the consequence of this has made service under him as a Cabinet officer difficult." Treasury Secretary Henry Morgenthau said, "The thing FDR prided himself the most about was 'I have a happy ship.' But he never had a happy ship."[73]

---

[70] David Halberstam, *The Best and the Brightest* (New York: Random House, 1972), p.92.

[71] Johnson, p.16.

[72] Ibid., pp.16-17.

[73] Robert A. Wilson, ed., *Character Above All: Ten Presidents From FDR to George Bush* (New York: Touchstone, 1995), p.18.

Roosevelt's system was thoroughly pragmatic. He likened himself to a football quarterback who doesn't know what the next play will be until he's seen how the previous one's turned out. Except in the administration of the war effort - where he delegated massive amounts of power to the generals - Roosevelt's technique was to divide responsibilities so he was the only player who knew all of the pieces. It was an inefficient but effective approach that took an enormous toll upon its practitioner. By 1944, forty-seven war agencies were reporting directly to Roosevelt. Photographs of FDR in his final days as president reveal not just an ill man, but an exhausted one.[74]

Kennedy had studied Roosevelt's system. He liked FDR's creative sparks, but he didn't like the in-fighting. He wanted to be in control of as much information as possible, but he didn't want to be physically drained. He felt the collegial management style would allow him to gain needed information in a non-manipulative manner that, due to its team-orientation, would be far less demanding.[75]

More so than Roosevelt, Kennedy fostered a personal, even a mysterious, style that elicited enormous loyalty from his associates. He had a small staff and, unlike FDR, didn't get upset if they garnered press clippings. There was no turnover among his major aides during his administration, despite the President's sometimes distant personality. An aide who'd worked with both Kennedy and President Lyndon Johnson recalled: "I must have had dinner with Johnson a hundred times and if you told me [senior advisor Theodore] Sorensen never once had dinner with Kennedy, I'd believe it. Kennedy was more reserved, a strange man, he never asked you for anything, but he got absolute loyalty. It reminds me of what Freud said, that the great leader is often aloof from other men."[76]

Right from the start, Kennedy created an aura that extended to his team and which eventually wrote a new chapter in presidential mythology. Long before management consultants Tom Peters and

---

[74] Johnson, p.35.
[75] Ibid., pp.124-125.
[76] Patrick Anderson, *The President's Men: White House Assistants of Franklin D. Roosevelt, Harry S. Truman, Dwight D. Eisenhower, John F. Kennedy and Lyndon B. Johnson* (Garden City: Doubleday & Company, Inc., 1968), p.197.

Robert Waterman initiated the "excellence" movement in the American workplace, President Kennedy launched a national excellence campaign. Whether talking about physical education programs, the arts or the intellectual caliber of his advisors, Kennedy extolled the virtues of the academically brilliant, the culturally aware and the physically fit. Although the 43 year old president came into office with no executive experience, he presented himself - and his youthful administration - as an exciting combination of visionary leadership and collegial management; one that produced a new breed of tough, pragmatic decision makers who eschewed ideology and organization charts and yet could be sensitive to human needs.[77]

Much of that posturing resembled resume' inflation. The Kennedy Administration contained an impressive number of Harvard graduates. Impressive, that is, until one realizes that Chiang Kai-Shek's administration proportionally had more prior to the collapse of China.[78] Speaker of the House Sam Rayburn brushed aside Vice President Johnson's description of the brilliant Kennedy team by drawling, "Well, Lyndon, you may be right and they may be every bit as intelligent as you say, but I'd feel a whole lot better about them if just one of them had run for sheriff once."[79]

Despite the undeniable qualities of the President and his appointees, the rhetoric surrounding this collegial band began to create a self-fulfilling prophecy. The Kennedy administration was extraordinarily macho. Although Kennedy was accused of "generational chauvinism" in his preference for younger appointees, his only real bias - aside from the sexism of the time - was in favor of veterans and toughness. In the jargon of the Kennedyites, there were "tough" and "soft" people and, as one aide put it, "Nobody in the White House wanted to be soft....Everybody wanted to show they were just as daring and bold as everybody else."[80] Historian Arthur

---

[77] Halberstam, pp.39-40.
[78] Theodore H. White, *In Search of History: A Personal Adventure* (New York: Warner Books, 1978), p.102.
[79] Halberstam, p.41.
[80] James T. Patterson, *Grand Expectations: The United States, 1945-1974* (New York: Oxford university Press, 1996), p.491; Thomas G. Paterson, ed., *Kennedy's*

Schlesinger noted that the administration "put a premium on quick, tough, laconic, decided people...."[81] Even the Peace Corps Director had a sign on his desk that read: "Good Guys Don't Win Ball Games."[82]

Along with this toughness was speed. An aide recalled that Kennedy's first comment was usually "What have you got?" or "What's up?" and then "You're supposed to tell him - bang, bang, bang." Diplomat George Ball recalled that Kennedy's style emphasized quick solutions, noting "...when one tried to point out the long-range implications of a current problem or how it meshed or collided with other major national interests, Kennedy would often say, politely but impatiently, 'Let's not worry about five years from now, what do we do tomorrow?'"[83]

Ultimately, this fast-paced collegial approach would lead to the United States becoming trapped in the quagmire of Vietnam. Critics would wonder how key decisions could have been made without considering what might transpire five or ten years in advance.

Here's how a management style helped to produce a foreign policy disaster. The collegial style's affinity for short-term results can be found in three events that punctuated Kennedy's foreign policy: the Bay of Pigs invasion, the Cuban Missile Crisis and the decision to support a coup against the leader of South Vietnam, Ngo Dinh Diem. The first was a short-term disaster, the second is generally regarded as a short-term crisis management success and the third nudged the United States onto a slippery slope toward long-term disaster.

It is important to consider the manner in which Kennedy preferred to make his decisions. His decision making was linked to his general approach to life. Biographer Richard Reeves noted:

"All his relationships were bilateral. He was a compartmentalized man with much to hide, comfortable with secrets and lies. He needed them because that was part of the stimulation: things *were* rarely what they seemed. He called people when he wanted them, for what he

---

Quest For Victory: American Foreign Policy, 1961-1963 (New York: Oxford University Press, 1989), p.15.
[81] Paterson, p.18.
[82] Ibid., p.15.
[83] Ibid., p.18.

wanted them. His children came at the clap of his hands and were swooped up and taken away at a nod to a nanny. After his election, he said his White House organization would look like a wheel with many spokes and himself at what he called, 'the vital center.'"[84]

He did not like Cabinet meetings - he thought them a waste of time - and was derisive of President Eisenhower's practice of having the full Cabinet voice opinions on narrow issues. Instead, he wanted specialized decision groups that could bring specific expertise to special problems. He dismantled much of Eisenhower's methodical foreign policy bureaucracy mechanisms and drastically reduced the number of formal meetings of the National Security Council. When he eliminated the Operations Coordinating Board, a group charged with processing foreign policy information to and from the President, he announced, "We plan to continue its work by maintaining direct communication with the responsible agencies, so that everyone will know what I have decided, while I in turn keep fully informed of the actions taken to carry out decisions."[85] This sounds reasonable on its surface, but as journalist Henry Fairlie observed, Kennedy did not seem to appreciate the value of opinions from nonspecialists, people who did not have a vested interest in the very framing of the problem. This practice excluded individuals who might have sufficient independence of thought to question the wisdom of increasing the American involvement in Vietnam.[86]

Kennedy's ad hoc approach to decision making produced disaster in the first 100 days of the administration during the Bay of Pigs invasion. The plan called for the United States to provide air support for an invasion force of anti-Castro Cuban exiles who were to land and spark a revolution that would ultimately free Cuba. The Eisenhower administration had approved the training of the exiles, but Kennedy reviewed the final plans and gave the order to launch the invasion. Although American air support had been promised, when the invasion force became trapped on the beach, Kennedy backed

---

[84] Richard Reeves, *President Kennedy: Profile of Power* (New York: Simon & Schuster, 1993), p.19.

[85] Ibid., p.52.

[86] Fairlie, p.137.

away from providing air support. The remainder of the force was captured, Castro's power was enhanced and the United States suffered a major embarrassment.

Kennedy reacted to the disaster by blaming the advice he'd been given by the Central Intelligence Agency and the Joint Chiefs of Staff, but his own desire for a quick fix to the problem of Fidel Castro had caused him to overlook obvious flaws. Prior to the invasion he'd met with former Secretary of State Dean Acheson. When Kennedy told him of the plan to land fifteen hundred Cubans against a possible Castro force of twenty-five thousand, Acheson expressed surprise that Kennedy was even considering such a plan.

"I've been thinking about it," Kennedy said.

"Well," replied Acheson, "it doesn't take Price-Waterhouse to figure out that fifteen hundred Cubans aren't as good as twenty-five thousand."[87]

After the disaster, one of his own Cabinet members hammered in Fairlie's point that often the best advice comes from unlikely quarters who don't have a vested interest in promoting a particular program. Arthur Goldberg, his Secretary of Labor, asked him why he hadn't gotten a broader range of opinion. Kennedy replied that Goldberg's area was labor, not foreign policy. Goldberg stood his ground. "You're wrong," he said. "You're making the mistake of compartmentalizing your Cabinet. There are two people in the Cabinet you should have consulted on this one, men who know some things, and who are loyal to you and your interests."

"Who," Kennedy replied.

"Orville Freeman and me." Orville Freeman was the Secretary of Agriculture; hardly on Kennedy's short list for advice on foreign policy. "Why Orville?" he asked.

Goldberg continued. "Because he's been a Marine, because he's made amphibious landings and because he knows how tough they can be even under the very best circumstances. He could have helped you."

"And why you?"

---

[87] Reeves, p.77.

"Because I was in OSS [Office of Strategic Services] during the war and I ran guerrilla operations and I know something about guerrillas. That they're terrific at certain things. Sabotage and intelligence, nothing like them at that. But they're no good at all in confronting regular units. Whenever we used them like that, we'd always lose all our people. They can do small things very well, but it's a very delicate, limited thing. But you didn't think of that - and you put me in the category of just a Secretary of Labor."[88]

Tapping the Cabinet's expertise wasn't the only thing Kennedy had not considered. In a post-disaster meeting with Dwight Eisenhower, the former president asked Kennedy about the process he'd used to make the final decision. "Mr. President, before you approved this plan, did you have everybody in front of you debating the thing so you got the pros and cons yourself and then made the decision, or did you see these people one at a time?"

Kennedy replied, "Well, I did have a meeting...I just approved a plan that had been recommended by the CIA and by the Joint Chiefs of Staff. I just took their advice." He went on to tell Eisenhower that he'd called off providing air support because he'd hoped to hide American involvement in the invasion. Eisenhower responded with skeptical questions: "Where did these people get the ships to go from Central America to Cuba? Where did they get the weapons? Where did they get all the communications and all the other things that they would need? How could you possibly have kept from the world any knowledge that the United States had been involved?"[89]

Later, Kennedy railed against the Joint Chiefs of Staff and the Central Intelligence Agency. In return, they held a low regard for the White House decision-making team. The Chairman of the Joint Chiefs called Kennedy's decision to withhold air support "absolutely reprehensible, almost criminal." The CIA operatives referred to the loose White House procedures as "the floating crap game."[90]

No one will ever know if the original plan had any hope of success. The President failed to recognize that his own changes in the

---

[88] Halberstam, p.71.
[89] Reeves, pp.102-103.
[90] Ibid., pp.72 and 103.

decision making mechanism - his own shift toward the collegial as well as an eagerness to sign off on a belligerent, tough, course of action and then change it once the exiles were on the beach - had played a major role in the fiasco.

What was born in the wake of the Bay of Pigs was the President's determination to get tighter control of the military by naming a new Chairman of the Joint Chiefs of Staff and to dilute the power of the Central Intelligence Agency's reports by bringing in outside advisors. He instructed his advisors to take more of a "generalist" view when considering issues, instead of just focusing on the specialties of their agencies and he made Attorney General Robert Kennedy and Senior Advisor Theodore Sorensen - his most trusted associates - special watchdogs to challenge future decision making sessions.[91]

He had a chance to try out his new system in 1962, when he learned the Soviet Union had put nuclear missiles into Cuba. What followed was a frenzy of collegial decision making that is an illustration of that style at its finest.

Kennedy convened the Executive Committee, or the ExComm, consisting of a wide range of top military and diplomatic advisors. He also brought in an array of outside advisors who were not reluctant to challenge the group's assumptions. In order to avoid influencing the debate, he left the room as the participants argued about the options and he went out of his way to protect dissenters from criticism, noting that he wanted to get all of the options out on the table.[92]

The product of these deliberations was a creative list of alternatives, ranging from doing nothing on up to full scale invasion. Kennedy eventually chose the middle range alternative of blockade, the Soviets agreed to withdraw their missiles in exchange for an American withdrawal of missiles from Turkey and the world's closest brush with full-scale nuclear war came to an end.[93]

Some later argued that the process had been less than successful because it gained a short-term victory at the expense of a long-term

---

[91] Johnson, p.138; Reeves, p.103; Patterson, p.496.
[92] Johnson, pp.143-147; Robert F. Kennedy, *Thirteen Days: A Memoir of the Cuban Missile Crisis* (New York: W.W. Norton & Company Inc., 1969), pp.30-33, 49-50.
[93] Johnson, pp.143-147; Reeves, pp.421-425.

one; that the Soviets put the missiles in Cuba to ensure the security of the Castro regime and that they pulled them out in exchange for just such a promise.[94] The collegial process also took a great deal of time. It may not have been feasible in a crisis that demanded a quicker response. The overall reaction, however, was highly favorable. When a president has kept the national honor and credibility while eluding a nuclear war, it is difficult to muster much criticism.

Was the Cuban Missile Crisis an aberration - a blip of success - or was it a turning point in Kennedy's management style? Did it signal that he had made the necessary adjustments and corrected the flaws in his collegial process? Or did it simply mean that the administration was prepared to deal with obvious short-term crises, but not the day-to-day decision making that eventually can lead to crisis?

The answer can be found in the decision that drastically deepened American involvement in Vietnam.

When Kennedy entered office, there were 675 American military advisors in South Vietnam, assisting the South Vietnamese in their attempts to stop an insurgency that was supplied and directed by the communist North Vietnamese. Ngo Dinh Diem, South Vietnam's president, was a Catholic in a Buddhist nation. He was authoritarian and headed a corrupt regime, although the corruption may not have been extraordinary by Asian standards. Diem was unpopular and aloof and saddled with an even more unpopular brother, Ngo Dinh Nhu, who headed the secret police and was regarded as a malevolent instigator of the Diem regime's oppressive activities. Student and Buddhist protests against the Diem regime resulted in increased repressive actions that in turn led to more protests.[95] By the time President Kennedy appointed Henry Cabot Lodge as Ambassador to South Vietnam, the situation had so deteriorated Kennedy remarked that Lodge might have to stand aside and watch as the military unseated Diem.[96]

---

[94] Paterson, pp.151-152. See also Daniel Patrick Moynihan's analysis contained in G. Barry Golson, ed., *The Playboy Interview* (Wideview Books, 1981), p.498.

[95] Francis X. Winters, *The Year of the Hare: America in Vietnam January 25, 1963 - February 15, 1964* (Athens: University of Georgia Press, 1997), pp. 40-53; Paterson, p.228; Reeves, pp.489-490; Patterson, pp.513-514.

[96] Reeves, p.527.

Kennedy's decision to put Lodge in a key position at a crucial time was both odd and unfortunate. Throughout their political careers, the two men had known one another as rivals. Kennedy had beaten Lodge twice: once when he took his Senate seat and again in 1960 when the Kennedy - Johnson ticket defeated that of Nixon and Lodge. Lodge was a blue-blooded Republican who'd served as Eisenhower's Ambassador to the United Nations. He was a general in the Army reserves, had served honorably during World War II, spoke French fluently and had studied American policy in Vietnam. For a Democratic president who wanted a bipartisan stamp on his Vietnam policy, Lodge seemed to be an ideal choice.[97]

He had, however, two pronounced weaknesses. First was his reputation as a man who was hard to control. While at the United Nations, Lodge had balked at taking instructions from the State Department, once even voting against the Department's declared policy. [As part of his agreement to serve in the Vietnam ambassadorial post, Lodge arranged a direct reporting channel to the President, rather than to the Secretary of State.] During the 1960 race, Lodge continued his independent ways, becoming known as a lethargic campaigner who was prone to taking naps in the afternoon. Robert Kennedy strongly opposed the ambassadorial appointment, telling his brother that Lodge was going to cause a lot of difficulty. Lodge's other weakness was that he was an intellectual lightweight who looked the part of the handsome and savvy diplomat, but was deficient in the areas of judgment and perspective. At a delicate point in the history of American involvement in Vietnam, President Kennedy had appointed an ambassador who was unreliable.[98]

Lodge arrived in Saigon on August 22, 1963. Less than three months later, he had shifted American policy away from support of Diem and had sparked a coup that toppled the regime. In doing so, he manipulated Kennedy's management system and set the stage for massive American involvement in Vietnam.[99]

[97] Winters, pp.37-38; Halberstam, p.260.
[98] Winters, pp.166-171.
[99] Winters, p.53; Reeves, pp.558-563.

The collegial management style requires high maintenance. It demands a great deal of time. Good faith on the part of its participants is also a necessity. John Kennedy was given neither time nor good faith collegiality in this decision. In fact, collegiality was supplanted by conspiracy. Here's how it happened.

There is one premise that most historians would agree upon: The South Vietnamese generals would not have launched a coup without a signal that the United States would recognize the new government. They could not risk succeeding in overthrowing Diem, only to find that the Americans were using the coup as a pretext for withdrawal.

It is also clear that the President was hungry for reliable information. His desire to be the hub of the wheel was being fulfilled in that enormous amounts of information were pouring in to him. The problem was that the reports were often conflicting. On one occasion, Kennedy sent some advisors on a fact-finding tour of South Vietnam and they returned with such contradictory views that he asked them if they had gone to the same country.[100] In order for his collegial system to work, Kennedy would need sufficient time to sort through the information mass and reach a conclusion.

But he didn't have the time because he'd authorized Lodge, who was eager to back a coup, to establish contacts with the South Vietnamese generals regarding their intentions. Lodge did so and sent a clear signal that the United States would not discourage or oppose a coup. Once that was done, Kennedy's collegial system was doomed. It required time and the tight control that was necessary to guarantee time. The minute the disaffected generals saw that the United States wouldn't resolutely oppose a coup, the initiative for future action passed from the Kennedy administration to them. Kennedy's information gathering could be interrupted at any time by the South Vietnamese generals.[101]

Lodge quickly moved out of control. He established an alliance with Undersecretary of State for Far Eastern Affairs Averell Harriman and the two plotted to persuade the President to back a coup. Opposing their efforts was General Maxwell Taylor, the Chairman of

---

[100] Reeves, p.595.
[101] Reeves, pp.563-565.

the Joint Chiefs of Staff and General Paul Harkins, the commander of
the American forces in South Vietnam, who felt that Diem was better
than any possible alternative.[102]

Kennedy's collegial system became one of conspiracy as both
sides - through cables, bureaucratic end-runs and back-stabbing -
sought to win the heart and mind of the President. After one
particularly embarrassing episode, the President exclaimed, "This shit
has got to stop." But it continued.[103]

On October 29, 1963, one of the President's watch-dogs, his
brother Robert, noted that he had not been included in the cables on
Vietnam and that he had some serious reservations about where the
administration was headed. He bluntly noted that the coup talk made
no sense because the United States would be "putting the future of
Vietnam and in fact all of Southeast Asia in the hands of one man not
now known to the U.S....."[104] It was clear from his remarks that
although the United States had given approval for a coup, it did not
know just who would hold power if Diem were removed. The
subsequent discussion revealed that the President did not understand
how disruptive such a change of government would be, since he
expressed surprise when informed that Diem's removal meant that
there would be a massive replacement of officials throughout the
country because of their status as Diem appointees.[105]

As a result of that meeting, a cable was sent to Ambassador
Lodge telling him not to encourage a coup. Lodge interpreted the
cable to mean that he should discourage coups that had a poor chance
of success. The White House again tried to rein in Lodge, apparently
thinking that coup plans can be turned about like sports cars, but it
was too late. The coup took place on November 1, 1963. Diem and
his brother were murdered by the generals, and a revolving door
series of South Vietnamese governments soon followed. John F.
Kennedy was assassinated on November 23, 1963 and Vice President

[102] Winters, pp.81-90; Reeves, p.607.
[103] Reeves, p.567.
[104] Winters, p.100.
[105] Ibid., p.101.

Johnson, who had opposed the overthrow of Diem, inherited the deteriorating situation.[106]

The collegial management style that had worked so well during the Cuban Missile Crisis broke down during the deliberations on Diem. The process achieved gridlock due to so much raw and conflicting information and was subverted the minute Lodge told the South Vietnamese generals the United States would back a coup. Its emphasis on the bottom line caused otherwise ethical men to ignore the likely implications of what they were proposing. [When Kennedy learned that the generals had murdered Diem, he grew ashen-faced and left the room. General Maxwell Taylor muttered, "What did he think to expect?"[107]] The long-range implications of the coup were not seriously examined until the last minute nor were the broader policy questions sufficiently considered.

The collegial management style is fragile. When it works - and it works best in small groups - it can be extraordinarily effective. The style, however, easily withers without large dosages of time and good faith.

COLLEGIAL LESSONS LEARNED

For many executives, the collegial is the most demanding of the three management styles. Although its informality will easily fit the democratic nature of today's workplace, executives should not adopt it casually because of its high maintenance requirements.

The greatest challenge for the collegial executive is learning how to bring some structure to a style that values the unstructured. That can best be achieved by guarding against the friction points where the management style has the potential to erode the leadership goals. Among the friction points are:

---

[106] Ibid., pp.102-107.
[107] Reeves, p.649.

Information Overload

The collegial quest for being at the center of things can result in information overload, where it is difficult to distinguish the reliable from the unreliable and the meaningful from the meaningless. This can produce instant paralysis or ignorant assumptions as the individual who has too much information is only slightly better off than the person who has none.

The standard advice is for collegial executives to have associates analyze proposed actions in a decision paper format that provides background, fairly describes all points of view and provides a wide array of possible options. The fact that the collegial executive wants a broad array of opinions and options doesn't mean that they cannot be considered in an organized fashion. The paper itself can be debated and thrashed about by a wide range of associates. [An excellent format can be found in a bastion of formalism, the United States Army, where the standard staff paper is organized into six sections: Problem, Assumptions, Facts Bearing On The Problem, Discussion, Conclusions and Recommendations.[108]] An important amendment for the informal and speed-happy collegial is for the author of the decision paper to include a section on who wasn't consulted. At least that disclosure will let the executive know which individuals or departments are being bypassed.

Hubris

The collegial environment's pragmatism can create a group hubris, where the executive and the associates see themselves as not just different from other groups, but as intellectually and/or morally superior: the best and the brightest, to use journalist David Halberstam's term. Political observers noted both of these attitudes in the collegial atmosphere of the Kennedy and Clinton White Houses, where ideology was deemed less important than having the "right"

---

[108] Gil Dorland and John Dorland, *Duty Honor Company: West Point Fundamentals for Business Success* (New York: Henry Holt and Company, 1992), pp.85-86.

people making the decisions. In such cases, the decision making process becomes both a tool and a tribal ritual of confirmation. Its drawback, of course, is that insufficient attention will be paid to opposing viewpoints and that those captivated by this attitude may have ethical blind spots. One of the common artifacts found by ethical archeologists as they sift through the rubble of executive scandals is the belief that since the executives were good people, individuals of unquestionable achievement, then their decisions must naturally be morally and intellectually sound.

To guard against hubris, the executive should bring in outside advisors, rotate staff, establish clear ethical standards and require everyone, regardless of rank, to abide by them. It is crucial that the executive lead by example and that there not be any indication that winning is to occur at all costs. This means that discussion of what can be done be accompanied by discussion of what won't be done so each major decision making meeting has its own "ethics clarification" seminar. It is mind-boggling to consider that the Kennedy administration officials calmly discussed the backing of a coup against the leader of South Vietnam without the President ever being directly confronted with the fact that the coup was likely to end in Ngo Dinh Diem's murder.

Stretched Schedules

The collegial management system requires a great deal of the executive's time, thus robbing from the time needed for rest and reflection. Because of this, the collegial management style is best used for special projects and not as a regular routine. If used too long, it will exhaust the executive and encourage him or her to rush through decisions in order to get past the problem.

Executives should strictly limit use of the collegial approach to special occasions that require extraordinarily fast decisions and when staffing the decision through the usual process just isn't feasible. For the majority of decisions, a formalistic approach should be followed because it is far less physically draining. [See the next chapter for an analysis of the formalistic style.]

"By The Way" Decisions

Due to the lack of screening, the collegial executive is especially susceptible to "by the way" requests for decisions that may be brought by well-intentioned associates or by manipulators seeking to avoid coordination with other associates or department. The associate's goal is to get a quick decision and once that is accomplished, he or she trundles on their way, oblivious to whether or not the decision will cause severe teeth-gnashing elsewhere in the organization. Sometimes, the instigator of the "by the way" decision is the chief executive. The effects are just as bad.[109]

With the exception of clearly minor items, the executive should drop every decision into the routine decision making process. This allows time for reflection on the merits of the proposal and also heightens the odds that the matter will be properly coordinated.

Inadvertent "Stacking"

The collegial executive can stack the deck by choosing advisors who are going to give a decision he or she favors. This may be done intentionally by "fake collegials" or inadvertently by executives who don't recognize their hidden bias.

Before finalizing a major decision, the executive should get critiques of the recommendation from individuals who are outside of the collegial decision making group. These individuals may be from other parts of the organization or from the outside. They can provide needed dissent and may - at the very least - give a broader perspective that will reveal how the proposed actions might be seen by people

---

[109] Samuel Kernell and Samuel L. Popkin, *Chief of Staff: Twenty-Five Years of Managing The Presidency* (Berkeley: University of California Press, 1986), pp.74-75.

who aren't as close to the decision. The primary qualification for such advisors is not a particular expertise in the subject matter, but instead a freshness of perspective, an independence of thought and the courage to give advice "with the bark off."

Short-Term Emphasis

The collegial executive's emphasis on pragmatism can wind up stressing the short-term and neglecting long-term interests.

This problem is difficult to address without sacrificing one of the collegial's style main advantages: speed. And yet the executive can require that every analysis include a section on "Potential Long-Term Consequences" which in turn can include a description of worst case scenarios. A common problem with many executives is not that they discount or underestimate dangers, but that they don't even acknowledge their existence. After the Exxon Valdez oil spill, the chief executive officer of Exxon seemed shocked that such a thing could happen. Even if a possible serious problem is surfaced, the executive might continue to downplay it if the problem cannot be visualized or if the decision maker senses that he or she has little control over the threat. That is why effective dissenters or those wishing to sound cautionary notes should always combine their positions with recommendations for specific action that can be taken by the decision maker. General warnings will not satisfy the collegial executives hunger for action.

Subverting the Rest of the Organization

The collegial teams and task forces may take an adversarial stance against the rest of the organization. Their prestige may weaken the morale of the professionals who have been excluded from the teams or task forces and may cause associates who have felt bypassed to shift their loyalties to narrower interests that may not coincide with those of the executive.

The executive should recognize that one person's "team" is another person's "inner circle." The collegial executive will have to make an extra effort to include input from non-team members and to build a broader consensus within the organization for the team's decisions. This may require that any special teams or task forces be used more as consultants to the rest of the organization in order to keep them from being seen as a counter-organization.

Disrupting the Chain of Command

As they seek to avoid filtered information, collegial executives often cut across lines of authority and bungee-jump down the chain of command to glean greater insight. Such "info raids" may disrupt the regular chain of command. They also can be perceived as a signs of mistrust by associates who have been bypassed. It can erode their authority and their ability to assist in the implementation of the project.

The executive should recognize that disruption is inevitable and that it is a price to be knowingly paid. At the same time, the executive should take action to assure the bypassed that their status has not been undermined. This is easier for executives who possess a charisma or vision that enlists their followers in a larger purpose or a noble cause. It is more difficult when the executive's relationship with the associates is more transactional, such as "I do this for you and you do this for me."

One of the reasons for some of the exclusion is the executive's simple ignorance of the capabilities of subordinate individuals and departments. If one is going to break through the bureaucracy and tap the resources of the organization, then it is important to know just where the resources are located. A departmental - and, in smaller organizations, individual - skills inventory can assist the executive in determining the available level of expertise.

Too Many "Tree Experts" and Not Enough "Foresters"

The collegial executive's tendency to use specialized task forces may prevent the unexpected insights that come from the involvement of non-experts. It also can fail to create the broad political base for acceptance of the policy within the organization.

As a safeguard, the executive should ensure that advisory teams have a healthy mixture of generalists and specialists. The executive should declare that resistence from different parts of the organization may have a sound basis and that resisters should not be labeled as troglodytes or reactionaries. Naming a "devil's advocate" to challenge the group's assumptions can help to legitimize dissent and bring possible drawbacks into the daylight.

Chapter 4

THE FORMALISTIC EXECUTIVE

Robert Reich, Secretary of Labor in the Clinton administration, once explained why that administration had "so many summits and policy by discussion." Reich said, "We're almost all the products of the sixties generation, in which the process of decision making is very different from the process of decision making of the generation that went before us - people coming out of the Second World War. And the revolts of the sixties were very much in reaction to the hierarchical society we inherited. So every time I feel exasperated by how decisions are made here, why so many people are in on them and why it's so hard to get closure, I've decided a lot of it is deliberate, not just at the White House, but in my own department as well. I'm much more comfortable making decisions sitting around a table with assistants than *sitting at a desk and checking a box* [emphasis added]."[110]

Reich's analysis contains two errors: (1) the Clinton administration, as the first non-Second World War veteran-led administration, was not the first to use collegial management; and (2) the formalistic management style does not consist of sitting at a desk and checking boxes.

---

[110] Elizabeth Drew, *On The Edge: The Clinton Presidency* (New York: Simon & Schuster, 1994), p.247.

Collegial executives, such as Reich, and autocrats, such as the Robert Maxwell-wannabes of the world, regard the formalistic management style as needlessly time-consuming. They believe it smothers creative leadership and paralyzes effective management. They fear its layers and steps become mazes where crucial information is bludgeoned and buried by manipulative staff members. Autocratic and collegial executives are especially scornful of this style, but then, a la Reich, they are often at war with hierarchy. They regard rigid structures, regulations and procedures as pillars of bureaucracy that need to be toppled or circumvented.

These criticisms are a bum rap. Unlike the collegial and autocratic styles, the formalistic management style does emphasize use of a chain of command. The executive relies upon information being carefully analyzed by associates in their respective areas of expertise and then presented along with proposed recommendations for action. But it does not prevent the executive from sitting around a table with associates and discussing matters; in fact, that's an important part of most formalistic systems. And there's nothing inherently inept or bureaucratic about a formalistic management style. When handled well, it can enhance the leader's abilities far more than the autocratic or collegial approaches because it - more so than the other styles - best resolves the conflicts between leadership and management.

Like the other styles, formalistic management has its problems. It can create barriers to effective leadership and management. Among its obstacles are:

The formalistic management style can be slow and unresponsive. It can be frustratingly bureaucratic since its emphasis is on developing the best rather than the quickest or most expedient solution. This goal sounds laudable, but it may fall prey to "systems people" who emphasize rules and procedures over people. These "impersonalities" frequently have little concern or idea of how their actions may affect the lives of others. To such bureaucrats, the system is far more important than the mission.

Even if the associates are not insensitive, however, the system itself can be frustratingly slow. Furthermore, the simple process of coordination can pressure individuals or departments to develop opinions or posture on matters that they had hitherto regarded with indifference. This can cause the process to slip into a situation where, as one leader put it, "Everything has been said, but not everyone has said it."

The formalistic management style can filter information and isolate the executive from the real world. If the executive is to be protected from time-wasting whiners and excessively lengthy memoranda, then someone must do the screening and determine who is heard and what is seen. It doesn't matter if the title is chief of staff or executive secretary or administrative aide, once a person possesses the ability to edit the executive's range of knowledge, he or she becomes extremely powerful.

After reviewing the management styles of a wide range of political and corporate leaders, I reached a surprising conclusion: the executive who was best at balancing the often conflicting demands of leadership and management was Dwight Eisenhower.

DWIGHT EISENHOWER:
THE SUCCESSFUL FORMALIST

Senator Daniel Patrick Moynihan was once asked what made President Dwight Eisenhower such a good politician. Moynihan replied:

"His devastating capacity to make his enemies underestimate him. The popular view of Eisenhower among educated Eastern people was that he was a boob. He talked in convoluted, involuted sentences that didn't parse when transcribed, unlike the rest of us, who like to think we come out in lapidary prose. It's very agreeable to think, He's not as smart as I am; that's what's the matter with him. It was probably a very agreeable thought to Eisenhower. That's the way people got their balls cut off."[111]

The underestimation of Eisenhower also extended to his managerial skills. He was said to be a detached executive who was more interested in golf than in governing; one who would, to use Robert Reich's phrase, sit at a desk and check boxes.

Not only did this picture ignore Eisenhower's background - the former general in charge of the invasion of Europe just might know a thing or two about management - it also ignored reality. There is a reason why after talking with the associates of nine presidents from Roosevelt through Reagan, historian Fred Greenstein found, "None of the nine groups is more unified than Eisenhower's in its admiration of its leader."[112] And that reason was Eisenhower's ability to blend his leadership and management skills.

The motto that Eisenhower kept on his desk in the Oval Office was "Suaviter in modo, fortiter in re" (Gently in manner, strong in deed).[113] The dual approach suggested by the motto was followed by Eisenhower after he became president. He was not a collegial nor an autocratic executive, once noting, "In war and in peace I've had no respect for the desk-pounder and have despised the loud and slick talker."[114]

Eisenhower wanted to build a team of competent people who could work together well. With a keen eye for strengths and weaknesses, he carefully evaluated the people to be named to his Cabinet. This was a skill he honed during the Second World War when he had to decide which commander to use for specific assignments. He sent one assessment to his immediate superior, General George Marshall:

"I doubt that I would ever consider [General George] Patton for an army group commander or for any higher position, but as an army

---

[111] Golson, Moynihan interview, p.497.
[112] Fred I. Greenstein, *The Hidden-Hand Presidency: Eisenhower As Leader* (New York: Basic Books, Inc., Publishers), p.ix.
[113] Ibid., p.57.
[114] Ibid., p.240.

commander under a man who is sound and solid, and who has enough sense to use Patton's good qualities without being blinded by his love of showmanship and histrionics, he should do as fine a job as he did in Sicily."[115]

His assessment of personalities was an integral part of his Cabinet-building. Eisenhower was wary of Cabinets in which each department head was an advocate for a narrow set of interests. He wanted his associates to take a broader view - to be specialists, certainly - but also to have a stronger commitment to the team.[116]

He achieved this by giving his Cabinet a higher profile and more of a collective role than that found in the collegial Cabinets of JFK and Bill Clinton. Eisenhower wanted his Cabinet to be a "policy body." This didn't mean that it would make policy or vote on policy or initiate policy. It meant that the Cabinet would discuss policy and serve as a sounding board. It would hear Eisenhower's rationale for reaching specific decisions and, on occasion, Eisenhower would reconsider a decision based upon the input received from the Cabinet.[117]

Eisenhower accomplished several things by taking this approach. He briefed his associates on what was happening in their administration and gave them a sense of his goals and frustrations. He subtly reminded them that they were part of a team rather than independent operators. He gained greater support from his Cabinet members - even from those whose advice he didn't take - because he took the time to get their opinions. And he gave Cabinet members the opportunity to hear about projects involving other Cabinet departments that might require their assistance or advice.

After his first year in office, Eisenhower wrote a small critique of his efforts in his private diary:

"[A]s now constituted, I cannot think of a single position that I could strengthen by removal of the present incumbent and appointment of another. By no means do I mean to imply that any

---

[115] Ibid., p.77.
[116] Ibid., pp.77-80, 115-119.
[117] Ibid., pp.114-115.

one of my associates...is perfect in his job - any more than I deem myself to be perfectly suited to my own! I merely mean to say that I have a good many years of experience in selecting people for positions of heavy responsibility, and I think the results so far achieved by this Cabinet and by other close associates, justify my conviction that we have an extraordinarily good combination of personalities....I think the individuals in the Cabinet and other offices like each other. At least, I can detect no sign of mutual dislike among the group. I know that I like them all; I like to be with them; I like to converse with them; I like their attitude toward their duty and toward governmental service."[118]

The entry's emphasis on personality was no coincidence. Eisenhower believed that personality was as important as ability when building a team. Friendship among team members was a particular goal. He once observed that "In dealing with problems, friends develop among themselves a natural selflessness that is the outgrowth of their regard for the other. Personal antagonism enjoys the defeat of the opponent - consequently objectivity and selflessness cannot be attained when it is present."[119]

Eisenhower's careful selection process gained additional importance because of his delegation technique. He gave general guidelines, but left great discretion to his cabinet officers. He didn't want to micro-manage nor did he want to see his time consumed by what could more easily be handled by an associate. When the Secretary of Defense tried to bring a relatively minor problem to the White House, Eisenhower replied, "Charlie, you run defense. We both can't do it, and I won't do it. I was elected to worry about a lot of other things than the day-to-day operations of a department."[120]

Eisenhower's critics, zeroing in on a potential flaw of the formalistic style, alleged that he delegated too heavily and as a result did not know what was happening in his own administration. Recent scholarship, however, has revealed that Eisenhower had a much tighter rein, that he was extremely well-informed and that he was

---

[118] Ibid., p.120.
[119] Ibid., 119.
[120] Ibid., pp.83-84.

willing to cut across the lines of his formal system when such action was needed.[121]

Eisenhower's approach has been described as "the hidden-hand presidency."[122] He had the formalistic management style which allowed him to delegate heavily, but he also had a cadre of aides who could brief him on not just the main proposals that went before him for decision, but also on background information and comments by specialists. Those aides could go straight to the President without being cleared by Sherman Adams, Eisenhower's powerful chief of staff.[123]

Sherman Adams, who was known as the "abominable no man" because of his abrupt manner, was reputed to be a strict gatekeeper who kept Eisenhower from knowing about various issues and who sent the President carefully-digested decision papers. But evidence shows that Eisenhower's aide system more than overcame any possible gate-keeping by Adams. Telephone logs also reveal that Eisenhower regularly worked the phones heavily for information and advice.[124]

Eisenhower's dual system permitted him to assume the prestigious "chief of state" role in the public eye while keeping his more controversial "head of the government" role in the background. What seemed to be extensive delegation to subordinates allowed him to use his associates as "lightning rods" to absorb criticism. That strategy required that the associate be perceived as having sufficient power to be independent and thus responsible for what he or she has done. As one historian observed, an aide who is known to be a lightning rod ceases to be a lightning rod.[125]

Eisenhower's relationship with his associates followed the simple rule that if they were kept on the job, that meant he approved of their performance. He did not bully or berate individuals. If he concluded that a person was not going to fit into his team or perform

---

[121] In addition to Greenstein, see also Stephen F. Ambrose, *Eisenhower: Soldier and President* (New York: Touchstone, 1990).
[122] The phrase is Fred Greenstein's.
[123] Greenstein, pp.101, 146-151.
[124] Ibid., pp.136 and 147.
[125] Ibid., pp.90-91, 239.

satisfactorily, he got rid of the individual. This was not only a good way of ensuring top performance, it also maintained the concept of the team. Those who worked for Eisenhower could be assured that he wasn't secretly upset with their performance or simply "carrying" them to avoid the upset of a termination.[126]

For the most part, Eisenhower followed a strict rule of not publicly discussing personalities. This was consistent with his strategy of remaining above the fray and it meshed nicely with his overall leadership goals. Once, while working with aide Bryce Harlow on a press release, Eisenhower said, "Now Bryce, that's a fine statement....Go ahead and issue it. I made one little change."

Harlow replied, "Well, sir, what's that?"

Eisenhower said, "I struck out the word 'deliberate.'" He continued, "This is an attack on a person. When you said it was deliberate, what he had done, you were attacking his motives. Never, ever, attack a person's motives, Bryce."[127]

Eisenhower's practice of not attacking motives and avoiding public discussions of personalities was not a sign of weakness. He once explained:

"This is not namby-pamby. It certainly is not Pollyanna-ish. It is just sheer common sense. A leader's job is to get others to go along with him in the promotion of something. To do this he needs their goodwill. To destroy goodwill, it is only necessary to criticize publicly. This creates in the criticized one a subconscious desire to 'get even.' Such effects can last for a very long period."[128]

Eisenhower's decision making technique relied upon his formal and informal information chains. Formally, he wanted decision papers, preferably on one sheet, with the options carefully analyzed, but he also wanted ample discussion. As he described it:

"I have been forced to make decisions, some of them of a critical character, for a good many years. And I know of only one way in which you can be sure you've done your best to make a wise decision. That is to get all of the people who have partial and

[126] Ibid., pp.42, 238.
[127] Ibid., p.73.
[128] Ibid., p.74.

definable responsibility in this particular field, whatever that may be. Get them with their different viewpoints in front of you, and listen to them debate. I do not believe in bringing them in one at a time, and therefore being impressed by the most recent one you hear than the earlier ones. You must get courageous men, men of strong views, and let them debate and argue with one another. You listen, and you see if there's anything been brought up, an idea that changes your own view or adds to it. Sometimes the case becomes so simple that you can make a decision right there. Or you may go back and wait two or three weeks, if time isn't of the essence. But you make it."[129]

That describes his process of making a decision, but it doesn't reveal his criterion for determining the best course of action. The standard was which one of the possible solutions to the immediate problem will best conform to the long term interests of the United States and at the same time be able to attract sufficient support in the country and the Congress.

That standard shows part of the strength of Eisenhower's use of the formalistic management style. He sought to consider long term interests and have substantial political and public support. His use of his Cabinet helped to uncover a wide range of perspectives; ones that might not surface via the autocratic or collegial approaches. That process of inclusion also helped him gauge the amount of support a decision might have within his own administration, on Capitol Hill and in the rest of the country.

Eisenhower bolstered this approach by getting even more information through his informal network: the individual aides reporting on the background of various decision papers, the extensive phone calls and reading. His informal channels helped him to elude the danger of being fed slanted information by his staff.

There is no indication that Eisenhower's formalistic style resulted in the president getting less useable information than presidents who have adopted the collegial approach. In fact, you can argue that he got more information. Kennedy was swamped with information while he was trying to decide what to do with Diem and while attempting to

---

[129] Ibid., p.246.

sort things out lost control of events and plunged the United States even further into Vietnam. Clinton's approach often seemed more chaotic than collegial. Churchill's autocratic style heavily depended upon the formalistic support of the career military and civil service. Eisenhower's dual-track management style gave him the best of both worlds: he had a system that carefully processed proposed solutions to problems, coordinated those solutions with a wide range of opinions and stressed, to the greatest degree possible, consideration of long term interests. He carefully selected a team based on ability and personality and, through his use of the Cabinet, fostered a team-orientation. And he used a back-channel system of aides to get information outside of the normal avenues.

Eisenhower's approach permitted him to maximize his leadership and management skills. He realized he didn't need to know all the details, just the important ones, and his management style clearly enhanced his leadership. If Eisenhower has jumped into the thick of the decision making process, he would have been transformed from CEO to senior staff officer. The distance he kept gave him time and perspective and helped to preserve the mystique of his leadership.

FORMALISTIC LESSONS LEARNED

Out of the various management styles, the formalistic style is the easiest one to use. If neglected, it usually produces less damage than either the autocratic or the collegial styles because its rules and procedures are less personality-dependent. Its "one size fits all" nature can be effectively utilized by the introverted and the extroverted, the charismatic and the charisma-challenged. Although less colorful than its cousins, the formalistic style is also less likely to put its user in the ditch.

Its drawbacks should not be overlooked. Among them are:

Vulnerability to Manipulation

The fear that the leader-manager may be unduly and unwisely influenced by the inner circle is as old as organizations. There is an ancient Asian proverb that it is better to serve under a vulture king that is surrounded by swans than under a swan king surrounded by vultures.[130] The last one to recognize such influences may be the executive.

The formalistic executive should open other communication channels to ensure that he or she is not being kept from unpleasant but important truths. President Eisenhower used a system of aides to accomplish that task. Several other approaches are also effective:

15-5 Reports

These are weekly reports that take no longer than 15 minutes to write and no longer than 5 minutes to read. Every person in the work unit turns a report in on Friday morning. The reports are only one page long and can be hand-written.[131] They have three sections:

Part I.   What I did this past week.
Part II.   This week, my morale is:
Part III.   I think our [team, department, office, company] would improve by:

Obviously, the chief executive officer of a company with 20,000 employees can't read all of the weekly 15-5 reports, but a sample wouldn't be a bad idea. Supervisors of smaller units may want to read all of the reports. It is a great way to spot when morale is sagging, when certain problems are starting to develop a pattern and when employees perceive that management is unresponsive.

[130] H.G. Dulaney and Edward Hake Phillips, *Speak, Mr. Speaker* (Bonham: Sam Rayburn Foundation, 1978), p.428.
[131] Paul Hawkin, "The Employee As Customer," *Inc.*, November 1987, p.21.

Management Hot Lines

Usually, these are 24 hour a day toll-free numbers. Employees and customers can call in and report problems or ask questions. In organizations that have experienced labor unrest, it might be wise to have an independent firm manage the line so that callers can be assured that their calls will be confidential.

Employee Retention Programs

Far too many executives watch valuable employees turn in resignations and never seriously explore why the person is leaving. Such information is especially important to the formalistic executive who risks isolation. Unless management has been longing for a person to leave, once a resignation is turned in the executive should sit down with the employee and Human Resources personnel to examine just why the person wants to go and whether anything can be done to persuade him or her to stay.

Management by Wandering Around

MBWA is only as good as its practitioner. We've all seen executives who walk through an office, say a few glib and condescending words to the workers, then depart with the impression that they've learned what's happening. Effective MBWAers take time, get to know people by name, and make it very clear that they want to hear about problems. Whenever someone is so bold as to actually surface a problem, the wise executive makes sure there is a swift and sensitive response; the type that sends the signal that management both listens and cares.

One formalistic executive I know keeps a family photo album on the coffee table in his office. It contains photographs and background sketches of all 250 of his employees. He regularly thumbs through the album and has, over time, learned the names of all of the people in his department. He knows that many associates are reluctant to speak to the department director and that his ability to call them by name is one small, but important, way to open communication.

Parochialism and Lack of Coordination

One reason for collegial cross-functional teams is the concern that in the absence of such teams, associates might only advocate the narrow perspective of their particular work unit. This is not a baseless fear. Some of the monster stories to emerge from the automobile industry describe situations where the engineers, the designers and the manufacturing crews failed to communicate with one another.

The use of a formalistic style does not keep the executive from, on occasion, using cross-functional teams. If parochialism is to be eliminated, the executive must establish the strict rule that failure to coordinate and failure to cooperate will be seen as major violations. Whenever an intentional infraction occurs, severe disciplinary action should be taken.

Wasted Time

At first glance, the formalistic management style does waste time. There are proposals to be coordinated, approvals to be obtained and procedures to be followed. General staff meetings are held and many in attendance may dearly wish they were elsewhere. What is not appreciated is how much time would have been wasted if such safeguards were not followed. Chrysler Chairman Lee Iacocca hit the bulls eye when he observed, "In conversation you can get away with all kinds of vagueness and nonsense, often without realizing it. But there's something about putting your thoughts on paper that forces you to get down to specifics. That way, it's harder to deceive yourself - or anybody else."[132]

---

[132] Lee Iacocca with William Novak, *Iacocca* (New York: Bantam Books, 1984), p.47.

The formalistic executive likes formal decision papers because when people put things in writing, they are usually much more analytical than the associate who simply wanders into your office, hallucinates about some topic, then strolls on out. Decision papers provide you, the executive, with the best of your associates' reasoning. It also saves time since you don't have to translate how one disjointed comment connects to another.

Much of the squandered time in a formalistic system occurs because people don't understand why the system operates and how to operate the system.

The executive should provide periodic explanations of the idea behind the system; namely, that the procedures aren't there for procedures' sake, but are present because if they are followed there is a greater likelihood - a likelihood, not a guarantee - that the decisions reached will be better.

In addition to providing the big picture, the executive must teach associates how to operate a formalistic system. Specific training on topics such as how to prepare a staff paper, how to coordinate ideas, brainstorming, crisis management, who shares jurisdiction and who has exclusive control will help to lubricate the formalistic process.

The Bureaucratic Rap

Any time you have a system that involves decision papers and levels of review, you can bet someone will call the arrangement "bureaucratic." Not only does that term imply that the system is slow, unresponsive and rigid, it also evokes the danger that over time associates will come to regard the system, which is supposed to be designed to achieve the mission, as more important than the mission.

Helmut Maucher, the CEO of Nestle's, is a formalistic executive. He admits, "I listen a lot, but I make the final decisions. I want a team with a leader, not a team as the leader." He sees his primary role as keeping the company focused on its strategy of "global thinking, local commitment" and so pushes to ensure Nestle's expertise is used in accordance with local market preferences. So if the American, the

Chinese or the Thai markets have different tastes, Maucher's philosophy is to use Nestle's centralized expertise to help adjust Nestle's to the locality and not vice-versa. As a result, Nescafe in Thailand is sold as a cold shake, not a hot drink, and its market share has rocketed.[133]

One of his associates describes Maucher's management style as "the invisible hand." (Shades of Eisenhower!) Maucher makes sure that his overall strategy is reflected in the company's daily decisions and that the process doesn't erode the mission.[134]

Maucher travels extensively, talks to employees at all levels of the company and carefully studies the local customs in each market. Throughout this, he is promoting Nestle's strategy and the values and insisting that the daily actions be consistent with both.[135]

CONCLUSION

Formalistic management is not a passive, bureaucratic style. It does not preclude the use of collegial task forces or teams, nor does it mean that the executive has to be isolated from the day-to-day workings of the organization. For most executives, the formalistic style provides the easiest forum for the reconciliation of leadership and managerial responsibilities. Its emphasis on procedures can seem to be excessively managerial and less in the realm of leadership, but in reality it is there that the two can most creatively mix. As James C. Collins and Jerry I. Porras found in their study of successful organizations, there is a great deal to be said for such mixtures:

"Thomas Jefferson, James Madison and John Adams were not charismatic visionary leaders in the 'it all depends on me' mode. No, they were organizational visionaries...They focused on building a

---

[133] Charles M. Farkas and Phillippe DeBacker, *Maximum Leadership: The World's Leading CEOs Share Their Five Strategies For Success* (New York: Henry Holt and Company, 1996), p.44.

[134] Ibid., p.43.

[135] Ibid., pp.62-64.

country. They rejected the good-king model. They took an architectural approach."[136]

The formalistic management style gives the executive ample opportunity to take the "architectural approach" while building or strengthening procedures that will further the mission of the entire organization.

---

[136] James C. Collins and Jerry I. Porras, *Built to Last: Successful Habits of Visionary Companies* (New York: HarperBusiness, 1994), p.42.

Chapter 5

LEADERSHIP'S ALLY

The ally of both leadership and management is the willingness to modify or sacrifice a leadership or managerial responsibility in order to further the long-term interests of the organization. This pertains to particular styles. It can even pertain to specific actions.

CHOOSING A STYLE

In order to achieve the most effective alliance between leadership and management, the executive must select a style that most closely fits his or her personal strengths, modify the style to accommodate the needs of the organization and then retain the flexibility to abandon temporarily, if need be, their style for one that is more effective.

Many executives employ adaptations of the various styles, using a formalistic approach for most matters, a collegial for some and the autocratic for emergencies. Such flexibility is wise. As we have seen, in fields as fluid as leadership and management, much improvisation is appropriate.

There are, however, two areas that should not be changed. First is the executive's persona or public image. What happens when an introvert suddenly becomes extroverted or an efficiency fanatic passionately embraces disorganization... other than organizational chaos and suspicions of insincerity? Styles may be altered, but never the persona. Referring to his image as the wartime savior of France, Charles De Gaulle once reflected, "There are many things I would have liked to do but could not, for they would not have been fitting for General De Gaulle."[137]

The second unshakeable element should be the organization's core values. They need not be complicated nor should they oppressive, but they must be constant. If the core values are seen as negotiable, then the organization has lost its benchmark.

Unlike values, styles are simply daily strategies and strategies can and should change to adjust to altered circumstances. Naturally, it is important to know when to lean one way or another. Here is a general road map:

Handling Crisis

The autocratic style can be effective during a crisis, but if used for extended periods it harms the organization by creating dependent associates, driving off independent thinkers and stifling dissent. Executives who are determined to be autocrats should set a rigid term limit on their service, then move on before their style produces more problems than it solves.

If non-autocrats are faced with an immediate crisis requiring fast action, they may want to use the autocratic style and then revert to their usual style once the immediate threat has passed.

Setting Goals

The collegial management style is time-consuming and can be difficult to maintain over the long-term, but it is excellent when goals need to be set. Its information-rich environment and seminar-like exchanges can help to surface creative alternatives that might be squelched or missed by the other styles.

---

[137] Richard Nixon, *Leaders: Profiles and Reminiscences of Men Who Have Shaped the Modern World* (New York: Warner Books, Inc., 1982), p.55.

The collegial style can also be effective in flattened organizations where the hierarchy is small or nonexistent and where the executive is more of a team leader than a division or department head. It will still carry the same tendency to swamp the executive with information and consume vast quantities of time, but in a smaller work unit those drawbacks will not be as debilitating.

Routine Decision Making

If the goals and the means are clear and there is not an immediate threat, the formalistic style is best. There are formal work units and their lines of authority are respected, decisions are carefully coordinated and recommendations for action are analyzed prior to their submission to the executive. The formalistic executive may choose the collegial approach for special projects, especially ones in need of extensive brainstorming, but will otherwise stick to the procedures.

Determining the Means

If the goals are clear, but there is a conflict over the means to achieve the goals, either a collegial or a formalistic approach can be appropriate. The executive should ensure that the decision making process considers expert opinion on the proper course of action. The executive will then have to reconcile the expert technical - or managerial - advice with the values - or leadership goals - of the organization.

AUDIT. ADJUST. ACT.

The process of reconciling leadership and management is a continous one. It is not done once and then forgotten because circumstances may call for a different style or the style may have gradually evolved from one form to another. For example, what once was a dynamic collegial style may have jelled into a slower formalistic one. Denial of reality may also be present. The executive who sees herself as a caring, open-minded formalist may be regarded by her associates as an order-barking autocrat.

Audit - Adjust - Act is the revolving cycle for reconciliation.

AUDIT

AWARENESS

ACT   ADJUST

At its core is Awareness: awareness of the ways in which management styles can clash with or erode leadership goals. Condensed, those ways are:

Autocratic Executives:

- Cause associates to suppress dissenting opinions and thus create a defective decision making process.
- Drive off talented associates.
- Use "acquiescence by appointment" and replace dissenters with compliant associates.
- Micro-manage and inadvertently encourage their associates to delegate upwards matters that could have been more efficiently handled at a lower level.
- Build their decisions around their own narrow world view which is shaped by their insensitivity to the perspectives of others.

- Fail to prepare possible successors and, by doing so, shorten the potential life span of their works.

Collegial Executives:

- Put themselves at the center of things and get swamped with information.
- Are susceptible - along with their associates - to a form of group arrogance or hubris.
- Find that their time is consumed by associates and meetings.
- Resist delegating because it would take too much time to explain all that they know.
- Are vulnerable to associates trying to get "by the way" decisions and circumvent coordination.
- Often engage in fake collegiality and succumb to "stacking" their advisory group with people who will either agree with them or be compliant.
- Tend to emphasize short-term solutions and ignore the long-term impact.
- Stress pragmatism and the "bottom line" and risk an "end justifies the means" mentality.
- Take an adversarial stance against the routine organizational rules and procedures and weaken the organization.
- Bungee-jump down the chain of command while conducting "Info raids" and in so doing disrupt the organization.
- Risk relying too heavily on the advice of relevant experts and missing the insight that can come from disinterested generalists.

Formalistic Executives:

- Are vulnerable to manipulation by associates who feed them filtered information.
- Risk isolation from the real environment of the organization.

- Overemphasize procedures and encourage parochial turf wars and lack of coordination.
- Create bureaucracies that are slow, rigid and unresponsive.
- Squander time by requiring strict adherence to rules and procedures.
- Can be too tied to hierarchy in a world of flattened and lean organizations.

Leadership is poetry. Management is prose. Their differences are significant, but so too are their similarities. By carefully blending their strengths and weaknesses, executives will engage the hearts, minds and best efforts of the entire team.

BIBLIOGRAPHY

Ambrose, Stephen E. *Eisenhower: Soldier and President*. New York: Simon & Schuster, 1990.

Anderson, Patrick. *The President's Men*. New York: Doubleday, Inc., 1968.

Bennis, Warren and Burt Nanus. *Leaders: The Strategies for Taking Charge*. New York: Harper & Row, Publishers, 1986.

Beschloss, Michael R. *The Crisis Years: Kennedy and Khrushchev 1960 - 1963*. New York: Harper Collins Publishers, 1991.

Bothwell, Lin. *The Art of Leadership*. New York: Prentice-Hall Press, 1983.

Broszat, Martin. *The Hitler State: The Foundation and Development of the Internal Structure of the Third Reich*. London: Longman Singapore Publishers Pte Ltd, 1981.

Bryant, Arthur. *Triumph in the West*. New York: Doubleday & Company, Inc., 1959.

Burns, James MacGregor. *Leadership*. New York: Harper & Row, 1978.

Burns, Thomas S. *Tales of ITT: An Insider's Report*. Boston: Houghton Mifflin Company, 1974.

Collins, James C. And Jerry I. Porras, *Built To Last: Successful Habits of Visionary Companies*. New York: HarperBusiness, 1994.

Colville, John. *Winston Churchill and His Inner Circle*. New York; Windham Books, 1981.

Chester L. Cooper, *The Lost Crusade: America in Vietnam.* New York: Dodd, Mead and Company, 1970.

Cronin, Thomas E. and Rexford G. Tugwell. *The Presidency Reappraised.* New York: Praeger Publishers, 1977.

Dallek, Robert. *Hail To The Chief: The Making and Unmaking of American Presidents.* New York: Hyperion, 1996.

Drew, Elizabeth. *On The Edge: The Clinton Presidency.* New York: Simon & Schuster, 1994.

Drucker, Peter F. *The Effective Executive.* New York: Harper & Row, 1967.

Dudley, Donald R. *The Civilization of Rome.* New York: The New American Library, 1962.

Durant, Will. *Caesar and Christ: A History of Roman Civilization and of Christianity from Their Beginnings to A.D. 325.* New York: Simon and Schuster, 1944.

Fairlie, Henry. *The Kennedy Promise.* New York: Dell Publishing Co., Inc. 1973.

Farkas, Charles M. And Philippe De Backer. *Maximum Leadership; The World's Leading CEOs Share Their Five Strategies For Success.* New York: Henry Holt and Company, 1996.

Fleming, Gerald. *Hitler And The Final Solution.* Berkeley: University of California Press, 1984.

Galthrop, Louis C. *Bureaucratic Behavior in the Executive Branch.* New York: The Free Press, 1969.

Gardner, John W. *On Leadership.* New York: The Free Press, 1996.

Gilbert, Martin. *Churchill: A Life.* New York: Henry Holt and Company, 1991.

Grant, Michael. *The Twelve Caesars.* New York: Charles Scribner's Sons, 1975.

Greenstein, Fred I. *The Hidden-Hand Presidency: Eisenhower As Leader.* New York: Basic Books, Inc. Publishers, 1982.

Greenstein, Fred I. "The Hidden-Hand Presidency: Eisenhower as Leader A 1994 Perspective," *Presidential Studies Quarterly*, Vol. XXIV, Number 2, Spring 1994.

Halberstam, David. *The Best and the Brightest.* New York: Random House, 1969.

Harris, Kenneth. *Attlee*. London: Weidenfeld and Nicolson, 1983.

Hawkin, Paul. "The Employee As Customer," *Inc.*, November 1987.

Hayward, Steven F. *Churchill On Leadership*. Rocklin: Prima Publishing, 1997.

Healey, Denis. *The Time of My Life*. London: Penguin Books, 1989.

Hennessy, Peter. *Cabinet*. Boston: Basil Blackwell, 1986.

Hess, Stephen. *Organizing The Presidency*. Washington, D.C.: The Brookings Institution, 1988.

Hesselbein, Frances, Marshall Goldsmith and Richard Beckhard. *The Leader of the Future*. San Francisco: Jossey-Bass Publishers, 1996.

Hesselbein, Frances, Marshall Goldsmith and Richard Beckhard, *The Organization of the Future*. San Francisco: Jossey-Bass, 1997.

Hilsman, Roger. *To Move a Nation*. New York: Dell Publishing Co., 1964.

Hunt, Sir David. "Churchill At Work." *Speech to the Churchill Society for the Advancement of Parliamentary Democracy*, November 29, 1990, Toronto, Canada. Copy in British Library, London.

Iacocca, Lee with William Novak. *Iacocca*. New York: Bantam Books, 1984.

Irving, David. *Hitler's War*. New York: The Viking Press, 1977.

Janis, Irving L. *Crucial Decisions: Leadership in Policymaking and Crisis Management*. New York: The Free Press, 1989.

Jay, Antony. *Management and Machiavelli: An Inquiry Into the Politics of Corporate Life*. New York: Holt, Rinehart and Winston, 1967.

Johnson, Paul. *Modern Times: The World From the Twenties to the Eighties*. New York: Harper & Row, 1983.

Johnson, Richard Tanner. *Managing The White House: An Intimate Study of the Presidency*. New York: Harper & Row, Publishers, 1974.

Keegan, John, ed. *Churchill's Generals*. New York: Grove Weidenfeld, 1991.

Keegan, John. *The Second World War*. New York: Viking, 1989.

Kernell, Samuel and Samuel L. Popkin. *Chief of Staff: Twenty-Five Years of Managing The Presidency.* Berkeley: University of California Press, 1986.

Kets De Vries, Manfred F.R. *Leaders, Fools and Impostors: Essays on the Psychology of Leadership.* San Francisco: Jossey-Bass, 1973.

Kets De Vries, Manfred F.R. *Organizational Paradoxes.* New York: Routledge, 1980.

Kets De Vries, Manfred F.R. *Prisoners of Leadership.* New York: John Wiley & Sons, 1989.

Kouzes, James M. and Barry Z. Posner. *Credibility.* San Francisco: Jossey-Bass Publishers, 1993.

Lamb, Richard. *Churchill As War Leader.* New York: Graff Publishers, Inc., 1991.

Lawson, Nigel. *The View From No.11: Memoirs of a Tory Radical.* London: Corgi Books, 1991.

Lewin, Ronald. *Churchill As Warlord.* New York: Stein & Day, 1973.

Maraniss, David. *First In His Class: A Biography of Bill Clinton.* New York: Simon & Schuster, 1995.

Neustadt, Richard E. *Presidential Power and the Modern Presidents.* New York: The Free Press, 1990.

Nixon, Richard. *Leaders.* New York: Warner Books, Inc., 1982.

O'Toole, James. *Leading Change: Overcoming the Ideology of Conflict and the Tyranny of Custom.* San Francisco: Jossey-Bass Publishers, 1995.

Paper, Lewis J. *The Promise and The Performance: The Leadership of John F. Kennedy.* New York: Crown Publishers, Inc., 1975.

Pascale, Richard Tanner. *Managing On The Edge: How The Smartest Companies Use Conflict to Stay Ahead.* New York: Simon & Schuster, 1990.

Paterson, Thomas G., ed. *Kennedy's Quest For Victory: American Foreign Policy 1961-1963.* New York: Oxford University Press, 1989.

Patterson, James T. *Grand Expectations: The United States, 1945-1974.* New York: Oxford University Press, 1996.

Peters, Charles and Nicholas Lemann. *Inside The System.* New York: Holt, Rinehart and Winston, 1979.

Peters, Thomas J. and Robert H. Waterman. *In Search of Excellence: Lessons From America's Best-Run Companies.* New York: Harper & Row, Publishers, 1982.

Pfeffer, Jeffrey. *Managing With Power: Politics and Influence in Organizations.* Boston: Harvard Business School Press, 1994.

Ranelagh, John. *Thatcher's People.* London: Fontana, 1991.

Reeves, Richard. *President Kennedy: Profile of Power.* New York: Simon & Schuster, 1993.

Reeves, Richard. *Running In Place: How Bill Clinton Disappointed America.* Kansas City: Andrews and McMeel, 1996.

Rehfeld, John H. *Alchemy of a Leader: Combining Western and Japanese Management Skills To Transform Your Company.* New York: John Wiley & Sons, Inc., 1994.

Renshon, Stanley A. *High Hopes: The Clinton Presidency and The Politics of Ambition.* New York: New York University Press, 1996.

Renshon, Stanley A. "Lost and Found? Clinton's Political Center." *Presidential Studies Quarterly,* Vol. XXVII, No.1, Winter 1997.

Ridley, Nicholas. *My Style of Government: The Thatcher Years.* London: Fontana, 1991.

Rosen, Robert H. *Leading People.* New York: Penguin Books, 1996.

Sampson, Anthony. *The Changing Anatomy of Britain.* New York: Random House: 1982.

Schlesinger Jr., Arthur M. *Robert Kennedy and His Times.* Boston: Houghton Mifflin Company, 1978.

Sereny, Gitta. *Albert Speer: His Battle With Truth.* New York: Alfred A. Knopf, 1995.

Shepherd, Robert. *The Power Brokers: The Tory Party and Its Leaders.* London: Hutchinson, 1991.

Shogan, Robert. *The Riddle of Power: Presidential Leadership From Truman to Bush.* New York: Dutton, 1991.

Sorensen, Theodore. *Decision Making in the White House: The Olive Branch or The Arrow.* New York: Columbia University Press, 1963.

Speer, Albert. *Inside The Third Reich.* New York: The Macmillan Company, 1970.

Taylor, AJP. *The War Lords.* London: Penguin Books, 1978.

Thatcher, Margaret. *The Downing Street Years.* New York: HarperCollins, 1993.

Toland, John. *Adolf Hitler.* New York: Ballantine Books, 1976.

Walcott, Charles and Karen M. Hult, "White House Organization as a Problem of Governance: The Eisenhower System." *Presidential Studies Quarterly,* Vol. XXIV, Number 2, Spring 1994.

Watkins, Alan. *A Conservative Coup: The Fall of Margaret Thatcher.* London: Duckworth & Co., 1991.

Wheeler-Bennett, John, ed. *Action This Day: Working With Churchill.* New York: St. Martin's Press, 1968.

White, Theodore H. *In Search of History: A Personal Adventure.* New York: Warner Books, 1978.

Wilson, Robert A., ed. *Character Above All: The Presidents From FDR To George Bush.* New York: Simon & Schuster, 1995.

Winters, Francis X. *The Year of the Hare: America in Vietnam, January 25, 1963 - February 15, 1964.* Athens: The University of Georgia Press, 1997.

Woodward, Bob. *The Agenda: Inside The Clinton White House.* New York: Simon & Schuster, 1994.

Woodward, Bob. *The Choice.* New York: Simon & Schuster, 1996.

Wren, J. Thomas. *The Leader's Companion: Insights on Leadership Through the Ages.* New York: The Free Press, 1995.

Zalenik, Abraham and Manfred F.R. Kets De Vries. *Power and the Corporate Mind.* Chicago: Basic Books, Inc., 1985.

ACKNOWLEDGMENTS

Most books are produced when a writer's modest whirlwind of activity is accelerated by the assistance of many people. This book has been no exception. My extraordinary business partner, Diane Sanders, was a key figure in this creative process as she is in all of my consulting efforts. No consultant ever had a finer colleague. Diane was joined by Robert Chiffelle and Dallas Porter-Stowe, both of whom provided fresh perspectives. Dr. Ralph Edwards facilitated my use of the British Library system and Denis Mack Smith generously provided thoughts on the workings of a dictatorship. The staff members at the British Library, the Hayden Library at Arizona State University and the Institute of Contemporary History in Munich were uniformly helpful. And a famous Hitler scholar, who will go unnamed, inadvertently inspired me by insisting that Hitler did not have a management style; a position with which I respectfully disagree. The person who provided the greatest assistance and inspiration, however, has been my wife and best friend, Mary Ann Wade. With a blend of insight and patience, she read every draft and argued every point while walking around hills of books and mounds of paperwork. Her support and criticism made this a better book.

ABOUT THE AUTHOR

Michael S. Wade is a partner with Sanders & Wade Consulting Inc. in Phoenix, Arizona. Prior to starting his consulting practice, Mr. Wade served as the Equal Employment Opportunity Administrator for the City of Phoenix and as the Command Equal Opportunity Officer for the United States Army Criminal Investigation Command.

Mr. Wade holds degrees in government and law from the University of Arizona. A popular speaker, he has taught classes on effective supervision throughout the United States. His diverse client list has included major corporations, small businesses, state and municipal governments and a professional basketball team.

Leadership's Adversary is his second book.

INDEX